"I have walked with Courtney [illegible] of times and been the personal witness of her true, unending faith in God. She is the real deal. If you are facing what feels impossible, I can say with complete confidence that Courtney's life and testimony as shared so vulnerably in *Still Standing* will give you the hope and courage you need to keep going no matter what you face."

Ruth Schwenk, author of *Jesus, Calm My Heart: 365 Prayers to Give You Peace at the Close of Every Day*

"When life grows dark and we experience anxiousness, doubt, and even fear, our tendency is to withdraw from others—even from God. Courtney knows this darkness, but she also realizes that anchoring your soul to Jesus will empower you to survive. Through this biblical and practical resource, you will dig deep into God's Word and discover confident hope for the future."

Karen Ehman, *New York Times* bestselling author, speaker, Bible teacher in the First 5 app

"*Still Standing* brought tears to my eyes as I read Courtney's words and recalled my own days of darkness. But those tears were quickly replaced with joy as she reminded readers how God cares so much, is always with us, and never leaves our side. God always has a good plan for us, despite our circumstances, and if you are longing to love life again and start seeing the light at the end of the tunnel, this book is for you."

Tracie Miles, Author Coaching Services, director of COMPEL Training at Proverbs 31 Ministries, author of *Living Unbroken: Reclaiming Your Life and Your Heart after Divorce*

STILL STANDING

Bible Studies from Courtney and WomenLivingWell.org

Ecclesiastes: Wisdom for Living Well

Ruth: God's Amazing Love for You

Making Your Home a Haven: A 4-Week Bible Study

Rest and Release: A 4-Week Bible Study

Slowing Down for Spiritual Growth: A 4-Week Bible Study

Delight in the Lord: A 4-Week Bible Study

Don't Let Go! Holding Onto God When You Feel Like Giving Up: A 31-Day Prayer Journal

Resting in His Presence: A 4-Week Bible Study on the Names of Jesus

Peace, Be Still Christmas Prayer Journal

Books of the Bible Study Journals

Numbers, Deuteronomy, Joshua, Judges, Ruth, 1 Samuel, 2 Samuel, 1 Kings, 2 Kings, 1 Chronicles, 2 Chronicles, Ezra, Nehemiah, Job, Psalms, Proverbs, Ecclesiastes, Isaiah, Hosea, Mark, Luke, John, Acts, Romans, 1 Corinthians, 2 Corinthians, Galatians, Ephesians, Philippians, and James

STILL STANDING

HOW TO LIVE IN GOD'S LIGHT WHILE WRESTLING WITH THE DARK

COURTNEY JOSEPH FALLICK

a division of Baker Publishing Group
Minneapolis, Minnesota

Published by Bethany House Publishers
Minneapolis, Minnesota
BethanyHouse.com

Bethany House Publishers is a division of
Baker Publishing Group, Grand Rapids, Michigan

Printed in the United States of America

Library of Congress Cataloging-in-Publication Data
Names: Joseph Fallick, Courtney, author.
Title: Still standing : how to live in God's light while wrestling with the dark / Courtney Joseph Fallick.
Description: Minneapolis, Minnesota : Bethany House Publishers, a division of Baker Publishing Group, [2024] | Includes bibliographical references.
Identifiers: LCCN 2023050003 | ISBN 9780764242397 (paper) | ISBN 9780764242816 (casebound) | ISBN 9781493445226 (ebook)
Subjects: LCSH: Christian women—Religious life.
Classification: LCC BV4527 .J6758 2024 | DDC 248.8/43—dc23/eng/20231214
LC record available at https://lccn.loc.gov/2023050003

Cover design by Jennifer Parker
Cover image by Shutterstock
Author photo © Kelly Roberts

The events described reflect the recollection of the author and may differ from others' recollections. Names and minor details have been omitted or changed in some instances to protect the identities of the people involved.

Baker Publishing Group publications use paper produced from sustainable forestry practices and postconsumer waste whenever possible.

24 25 26 27 28 29 30 7 6 5 4 3 2 1

To my children, Alex and Alexis—

Part of telling my story is telling your story.
Thank you for sharing your story.
You have walked through the darkness
and are standing strong in the light.
I am so proud of you.
I love you both to the moon and back.

CONTENTS

INTRODUCTION

In the Beginning

> In the beginning God created the heavens and the earth. Now the earth was formless and empty, **darkness** was over the surface of the deep, and the Spirit of God was hovering over the waters. And God said, **"Let there be light,"** and there was light.
>
> Genesis 1:1–3 NIV, emphasis added

Darkness is aggressive. Darkness seeks to take space in every crack and crevice that it can find, and when darkness creeps into our lives, our faith can be shaken. Discouragement can settle in as we wonder where God is amid life's struggles and pain. This is when the walk of faith turns into a day-by-day decision.

We cannot be passive with darkness. The light must push back the darkness and shine into all those dark spaces where we hide in our hurt. But how do we push away the darkness?

> In the beginning was the Word, and the Word was with God, and the Word was God. He was with God in the beginning. Through him all things were made; without him nothing was made that has been made. In him was life, and that life was the light of all

> mankind. **The light shines in the darkness, and the darkness has not overcome it.**
>
> John 1:1–5 NIV, emphasis added

God has not left us alone to fight life's battles. He sent his son, Jesus, to be the light of the world. We must follow Jesus. He will lead us out of darkness into the light. But let me forewarn you—sometimes light hurts.

Have you ever been in a movie theater for a long time, and when you came out into the hallway you pulled back and squinted your eyes? In time your eyes adjusted so you could see clearly, but in the moment, the light hurt. The light hurt because you had grown comfortable in the darkness. The enemy wants you to be so comfortable that you have no desire for the light. But the light is good.

We know the light is good, but living in the light can be hard when you wonder where God is and why he is not answering your prayers. Living in the light can be hard when you are following God's way and yet your dreams are fading away. Living in the light can be hard when his Word says all things work together for good, and yet you know what you are facing is clearly not good at all.

I wrote this book for every woman who has struggled to find peace when there is none or to find joy when life is not enjoyable. I've been there, and I do not want us to just fake fine; I want us to be victorious! I want us to find strength in our faith and keep standing. And I want us to do more than stand; I want us to take hold of the abundant life that Jesus promises in John 10:10 (NIV): "The thief comes only to steal and kill and destroy; I have come that they may have life, and have it to the full."

Some of our struggles are the same and some of them may be different, but ultimately we all face life struggles. Perhaps you are wrestling today with a wayward child or the betrayal of a close friend. Maybe you are struggling with a financial strain or a serious health problem and fear is gripping your heart today. Perhaps your marriage is harder than you ever imagined it would be, or worse, it is falling apart. Maybe your in-laws continually hurt you, or you have a boss at work who does not recognize your value and you wonder if you should stay or go. Oh, friend, my heart breaks for the losses you have suffered. I know so many have suffered the death of a mother, a father, a child, or a dream.

The enemy is real. The Bible says he is like a roaring lion seeking whom he may devour, and I am not about to let you be devoured! I want to fight alongside you.

I have wrestled in the dark while living in God's light, and I am ready to share some of the darkest seasons of my life with you in hopes that you will find hope, not from me but from the Lord. We are going to visit some of the emotions the enemy uses to hold us in a headlock—emotions like anger, sadness, fear, embarrassment, and worry. And we are going to talk about grief, loss, and healing your wounds so you can find rest.

We may be fighting different battles, but we serve the same mighty God who is stronger than the enemy! And so when fear, anxiety, and darkness press in, when you start out the day thinking it will be different, but by the end of the day you are knocked down again and wondering if this season of life will ever end, I want you to know you are not alone.

The only way out is through. I've been through, and I know without a shadow of a doubt that there is light at the end of the tunnel. That's why I wrote this book. This is my story of healing and my recollection of the events in my life. My hope and prayer is that it would be like a flashlight or a tiny torch with a flickering flame to help you walk through the dark tunnel you are in right now. So let's walk through together.

Let's get up for the hundredth time after the enemy has knocked us down . . . again.

Let's rise to the challenges that are set before us and endure our hardships and afflictions to the glory of God . . . again.

Let's remember our hope is in the one who rose from the dead and who assures us that one day we too will rise with him and spend eternity in heaven with him, where there is no more pain and no more tears.

This is our sure hope and our firm foundation that we stand upon. "Therefore, my dear brothers and sisters, stand firm. Let nothing move you" (1 Corinthians 15:58 NIV).

PART 1

WHEN GOD SEEMS SILENT

1 I cried out to God for help;
I cried out to God to hear me.
2 When I was in distress, I sought the Lord;
at night I stretched out untiring hands,
and I would not be comforted.

3 I remembered you, God, and I groaned;
I meditated, and my spirit grew faint.
4 You kept my eyes from closing;
I was too troubled to speak.
5 I thought about the former days,
the years of long ago;
6 I remembered my songs in the night.
My heart meditated and my spirit asked:
7 "Will the Lord reject forever?
Will he never show his favor again?
8 Has his unfailing love vanished forever?
Has his promise failed for all time?
9 Has God forgotten to be merciful?
Has he in anger withheld his compassion?"

[10] Then I thought, "To this I will appeal:
the years when the Most High stretched out
his right hand.
[11] I will remember the deeds of the LORD;
yes, I will remember your miracles of long
ago.
[12] I will consider all your works
and meditate on all your mighty deeds."

[13] Your ways, God, are holy.
What god is as great as our God?
[14] You are the God who performs miracles;
you display your power among the peoples.
[15] With your mighty arm you redeemed your
people,
the descendants of Jacob and Joseph.

[16] The waters saw you, God,
the waters saw you and writhed;
the very depths were convulsed.
[17] The clouds poured down water,
the heavens resounded with thunder;
your arrows flashed back and forth.
[18] Your thunder was heard in the whirlwind,
your lightning lit up the world;
the earth trembled and quaked.
[19] Your path led through the sea,
your way through the mighty waters,
though your footprints were not seen.

[20] You led your people like a flock
by the hand of Moses and Aaron.

Psalm 77 NIV

1 | Where Are You, God?

I sat in my car, stunned and in utter disbelief, but trying my best to keep up our family's routine for the sake of my two young children. Just five days earlier, I'd thought my life as a woman, wife, and mom was completely fine. Happy, even. But then it all came crashing down.

Out of nowhere, my husband of nearly two decades suddenly and unexpectedly walked out the door to start a new life with someone else. My kids and I had stood there shocked and confused, not knowing what to do next.

How can he do this? I'd thought to myself. *Christmas is in just three days! How are we going to celebrate? Do we even celebrate? How do I tell my family? We are going to have to tell his family. But wait—do they already know?* My mind had pondered if it could all be fixed somehow. Maybe I could cover for him and say we'd just had a fight. But no. He'd said I was to tell them the truth—that he'd left. So I did.

First, I called my parents with the devastating news. Then I texted his brother. And just like that, the ripple effect of my life being torn apart began.

Christmas came and went. It was the Sunday after Christmas. As usual, the kids and I went to church. I dropped them off at the door to go into youth group, and then I drove to the parking lot of a nearby hotel and laid my seat back in the car. I attempted to close my eyes to get a few minutes of sleep while fighting back tears. I was determined to not mess up my makeup, but I was exhausted. Physically, emotionally, mentally, and spiritually exhausted.

As I lay there in the car, rain poured down over my windshield as the weather reflected my pain and sorrow. In just one short hour, I would have to walk into the worship service without my husband—the man who'd sat beside me in the pew for over twenty years—and attempt to act normal. I had this massive secret that I was going to have to try to hide.

And hide I did.

I walked through those church doors and put on the best Sunday-morning smile I could muster. Friends came up to me and hugged me, asking how my Christmas had been. My mind raced. "Busy, I'm exhausted," I answered. Then I sat there and appeared to listen to the sermon. However, I did not hear a word the preacher said. My only goal was to get out of that building before someone figured out my huge secret.

When life hurts, sometimes we hide. And when we hide and get isolated, the darkness moves in. And when the darkness moved into my life, a wrestling match like I've never experienced—between the light and darkness—began.

And so this was the beginning of the darkest season of my life. I had lived life in the light and fought wrestling matches in the dark before, but none compared to what I was about to face. I'll share more of this story with you as we move through this book, but I want you to know this: if you find yourself in some kind of darkness right now—in your family, with your health, in your workplace, in your community—even in the silence, God is with you.

Ephesians 6:12–13 says, "We do not wrestle against flesh and blood," but instead, it says we wrestle "against the rulers, against the authorities, against the cosmic powers over this present darkness, against the spiritual forces of evil in the heavenly places. Therefore take up the whole armor of God, that you may be able to withstand in the evil day, and having done all, to stand firm." *Stand.*

Our opponent is not a person. Our battle is not a physical one. We fight an unseen enemy not with weapons or punches but spiritually through our spiritual armor and standing firm on the Word of God.

Our enemy is Satan, and he is not to be underestimated. He is evil. He is skilled at deception, and so in times of loss, death, divorce, and other life struggles, even the strongest believer may ask God *Where are you?*

Paul tells believers in Ephesians 6 that when the darkness presses in, take up the whole armor of God and stand. Keep standing! But how do we stand when we can't even get out of bed? Or when we are out of bed and standing, but our mind is racing with fear, sadness, pain, and sorrow?

I have sat and reflected on the messes in my life and wondered where God could be found. The hope of God swooping in and fixing certain problems, which I knew he could do, did not happen.

If you have felt this feeling before, it can be intensely painful. Be aware: this can be a trap of our enemy. He wants us to believe that God does not care. He wants to keep us stuck in our pain. He does not want us to live free or to experience the abundant life that Jesus says he gives: "The thief comes only to steal and kill and destroy. I came that they may have life and have it abundantly" (John 10:10).

God Cares

In Matthew 5, there were crowds all around Jesus, and so he went up on a mountain and sat down and began to teach them.

In the middle of his sermon, he said, "Therefore I tell you, do not worry about your life, what you will eat or drink; or about your body, what you will wear. Is not life more than food, and the body more than clothes?" (Matthew 6:25 NIV).

This was a profound teaching. Many in the crowd that day were poor, and yet Jesus told them not to worry about their food, drink, body, or clothing. Why? Because he wanted them to trust him to provide.

And so he told them, "Look at the birds of the air; they do not sow or reap or store away in barns, and yet your heavenly Father feeds them. Are you not much more valuable than they?" (Matthew 6:26 NIV).

Look at the Birds

Birds are not farmers. They do not plant their food, they do not harvest their food, and they do not have barns to store their food. There are an estimated fifty billion birds alive in the world today,[1] and every single day God feeds them all! Jesus says your heavenly Father values you much more than the birds.

Does this mean that food is going to show up on your doorstep every day? No. Look at the birds. Watch them. They are busy. They are always on the move, working to collect the provision God has for them.

They are not worrying.

They are living one day at a time.

One Day at a Time

When I was married, nearly all of the things we owned and all of the bills were in my husband's name. This was a blessing until he was gone and I suddenly had access to nothing. We had a savings account, a retirement account, and we owned some businesses, but I had access to none of it. For the next year and a half, I would have nearly no money in my one little bank account as I lived from month to month, and because my name was on nothing, I had no credit to my name. I didn't realize how big a problem this was until I went to the bank and opened an account in my name and attempted to get a credit card.

I was declined.

I explained my situation to the sweet lady at the bank. She looked at me with sad eyes and advised me to get a prepaid card and work on building up my credit score. I sat there in disbelief. I was forty years old with no credit to my name. I was a homeschool mom with no steady income. My writing online was simply a hobby, and any income I had from writing I had not saved but rather donated to other ministries.

Life was quickly becoming downright scary.

Jesus's words from Matthew 6:25–26 came to mind:

> "Do not worry."
> "Look at the birds."
> "Are you not much more valuable than they?"

I was worried. The darkness was coming for me. My mind began to race with how I was going to fix this problem, and so I did the only thing I knew to do—I cried. Then I prayed, and I begged the Lord to help me. And then I put one foot in front of the other, and like the birds, I began to work. I found ways to make an income while still homeschooling my kids, and I worked on building up my credit with my little $300 prepaid card. I would continue to purposely use that card to prove I could pay my bills, until one day I got a notice in the mail that I no longer had to prepay and now had a limit of $600 on the card. That was a happy day! I was doing it! One day at a time, God was providing.

A few years later, I went to buy my daughter her first car for her sixteenth birthday. The salesman at the car dealership ran my credit, and he said in a surprised tone, "You have an excellent score, but your credit is shallow." I just smiled and nodded my head.

My finances were not fixed in a day nor was my worry. It was a journey and a wrestling match in the dark as I battled between trusting God and living in fear, but this I can testify: every day God was faithful.

Where Is Your Faith?

In this same passage of Scripture, Jesus says,

> Why do you worry about clothes? See how the flowers of the field grow. They do not labor or spin. Yet I tell you that not even Solomon in all his splendor was dressed like one of these. If that is how God clothes the grass of the field, which is here today and tomorrow is thrown into the fire, will he not much more clothe you—**you of little faith?**
>
> Matthew 6:28–30 NIV, emphasis added

We cannot put our trust in someone we do not know well. The deeper we know God, the more we will trust him. The deeper we know God, the less we will act like the world. Many run after all the things this world offers, and if we decide to run after those same things too, we have a lot to worry about because everything in this world is temporary. Most of it is here today and gone tomorrow. These things will always be slipping through our fingers, and we will come up empty and frustrated day after day after day.

God wants more for us.

And so Jesus says, "Seek first his kingdom and his righteousness, and all these things will be given to you as well" (Matthew 6:33 NIV).

God Already Knows What You Need

Since 2008, I have been writing online. At the end of every blog post, I sign it, "*Walk with the King.*" You see, life was not perfect back in 2008. There were plenty of stressors in my life as a newlywed and then as a new mom. My firstborn was strong-willed and a challenge in many different ways. Then balancing two kids and a husband who traveled for work was not easy either. I desperately needed God every day, and I knew that there was no higher priority in life than having a daily walk with the King of Kings and Lord of Lords.

Looking back, I can see that God was preparing me for the darkest season of my life. We have a heavenly Father who knows our needs. He knows we need less of what this world offers and more of him. So how do we seek his kingdom? By seeking the King of the kingdom.

The King of Kings offers us a worry-free life, but there is a condition: we must seek him first. When we surrender our time to God and spend it with him, we grow closer to him.

As we grow, the light shines into the darkness of our lives and the darkness is forced to leave. But before the darkness leaves, often there is a battle. No one lives in victory 24/7. We all get knocked down, but Ephesians 6 says to stand firm.

Oh, I know how hard it is to get back up again and stand firm when we feel tired, beaten down, and wonder how many more times we can get knocked down and stand up again. So how are we to live when we are still standing but discouraged? That's what this book is all about.

Jesus says, "Therefore do not worry about tomorrow, for tomorrow will worry about itself. Each day has enough trouble of its own" (Matthew 6:34 NIV). We can live victorious just one day at a time. The past may discourage you, and the future may worry you, but just for today, live in the moment. Tomorrow is not here yet, so do not borrow tomorrow's troubles and turn them into today's issues. Trust that God will give you the strength you need to stand today, and trust that God will give you the strength to keep standing tomorrow.

Now, seek God first. Be strong in the Lord, and together let's take it one day at a time as we walk with the King.

REFLECTION QUESTIONS

At the end of every chapter, you will find a set of five reflection questions. These can be used in three different ways. 1) If you are a reader and simply want to read through the book, you can read through the questions and reflect on your answers as you read them. 2) If you are a journaler, grab a notebook and take notes. Write your answers in your journal and any other thoughts that God brings to mind as you read each chapter. 3) Use these questions as discussion questions for your Bible study group or book club.

1. Read Psalm 77 again starting on page 15. Notice how the psalmist goes from feeling forgotten by God to praising God for his greatness and strength. What happened in verses 10, 11, and 12 that changed his perspective?

2. Now think back and remember the ways God has worked in your life in the past. Write down a few things he has done for you. Meditate on these things for a moment. How does remembering and meditating strengthen your faith as you face today's troubles?

3. Jesus made it clear in Matthew 6:25 that we are not to worry about food, drink, body, or clothing. Which of these do you think about the most and why? Has the

enemy gotten a foothold in your life in any of these areas and caused you to worry?

4. In what ways can you combat your worry by seeking God first in your life?

5. Are there any other areas where you feel the enemy is attacking you? List them. Now commit this list to the Lord in prayer, asking specifically for more faith today.

2 Does God Hear My Prayers?

I slipped into the booth across from one of my dearest friends, and quickly we went deep into conversation. We began sharing back and forth all the things that were weighing us down, and at one point she explained how discouraged she was feeling. She had been praying faithfully for years for the healing of a family member, and God had not answered her prayer the way she had hoped. I had prayed alongside her for years, and she was right. It seemed like we had prayed forever for things to turn around, with no changes in sight.

I shared similar discouragement. It had been a year and a half since my husband said he was leaving, and I had been praying and fasting over the restoration of my marriage again. God did not do what I had hoped during that time of intense prayer, and worse, it felt like my problems were multiplying daily.

We both sat there defeated as we wondered, *Why is God not answering our prayers?* We love God and serve him. We love others and serve them. We have hearts to obey the Lord, but in these areas of our lives we were met with silence from God.

Have you been there?

Perhaps you are single, and you have prayed for years for a godly man to come into your life, and there is no knight in shining armor in sight. Or maybe you married your knight in shining armor, but now your marriage is more difficult than you ever imagined, and you are praying your husband changes, but he is not changing.

Perhaps you long for children and have prayed for years over your infertility, with no answers, or you have a wayward child and are praying for them to turn their life around.

Perhaps you suffer with a chronic illness, and you are praying for relief. Or maybe you have struggled financially, and you have prayed for years for the Lord to provide breathing room in your budget, but you are still living month to month or, worse, a month behind.

Push Out the Darkness

When we have been praying for long periods of time and God does not seem to be answering, this is when the darkness presses in. The enemy begins to whisper lies to us, inviting us to think that perhaps God does not even hear our prayers or God does not love us.

The enemy wants you to feel alone and to stop praying. He wants you to give up. He wants to keep you stuck in his darkness and confusion. He wants you to lose your faith and joy.

Don't believe his lies.

I have journals full of prayers I prayed during my separation with my husband. At the time, it felt like none of them were being answered, and yet now I can reread my journals many years later and clearly see the hand of God in my life. I see that God answered some of my prayers with a clear *no*. And to be honest, I don't like to be told no. But I also see how when I cried out to God and said, "Lord, help me. Lord, sustain me. Lord, please provide. Lord, give me wisdom. Lord, protect my children, and, Lord, give me the strength for another day," God heard my cries.

Relief was not always immediate. I'll write more about that in coming chapters, but in time the Lord did help me, he did sustain me, he did provide, he did give me the wisdom I needed, he did protect my children, and he did give me the strength to stand another day.

Let me assure you, God hears your prayers.

God Is For You

I grew up in a strong, loving Christian home. My parents lived out their faith every day, and they taught me and my sisters how to walk with the Lord. But it wasn't a perfect home, where my parents told us what to do and we girls just obediently did all that they asked. Well, we did have one sister who was like that, but for me and my oldest sister there were attitudes and debates and some pushing back against the rules.

There were times when I felt my parents were the strictest parents in the world, and I would tell my parents this with the hope of changing their minds, but it didn't seem to bother them or make them waver in the slightest. They loved me too much to let me run amok, and this made me feel secure. I knew I was loved.

I did not always understand my parents' ways, but one thing I always knew was that my parents were for me. They could see the big picture, and so everything they did was out of their love for me. Sometimes we don't understand God's ways, but one thing we can be sure of is God is for us and he loves us.

God Sees Every Tear That Falls

In Psalm 56, David was on the run from his enemies, and sleep was not coming easily for him. Instead, he was tossing and turning and crying at night, and he wrote this about God:

> You have kept count of my tossings;
> put my tears in your bottle.

Are they not in your book?
Then my enemies will turn back
in the day when I call.
This I know, that God is for me.

Psalm 56:8–9

David knew that God saw his sleepless nights.

David knew that God saw every tear that fell.

And David knew that even though he was in deep distress . . . God was for him.

Friend, I do not know what difficulties you are facing today or how many tears you have cried or how many sleepless nights you have faced, but this I know—God is for you!

One of the Hebrew names of God is *El Roi*, which means the God "who sees."[1] This name was first used by Hagar in Genesis 16, when she was running from Sarai. She was fearful and all alone with her son, and it was in this dark place that God made his presence known to her. She was comforted by knowing that God saw her.

But What about Your Tears?

I did not used to be one who cried very often openly. My friends and family would tell you they rarely saw me cry until after my husband left me, and then I literally could not control my tears. I cried at family dinners, at coffee nights with my girl friends, at church during worship times, at the grocery store, at the bank, at the gym, and then in private too, like in my car, bed, and shower. You name the place, and I probably cried there. I was so raw during that first year that my tears came at the most inopportune times.

It was a very humbling time, and yet God used those tears. While the darkness seemed to swallow me up as I cried, there was strength on the other side of my tears. I often felt so much better after a good cry. God taught me it's okay to cry. God created us with tear ducts so we could express emotions that words cannot express. And, friend, I want to remind you your tears are safe with Jesus.

As we read through the book of Psalms, we see David crying out to God over and over and declaring that God is his refuge, his strength, his rock, and his unshakable fortress. That is our God! He is our refuge and strength. We can trust him through every valley and struggle. God is for you.

Tears are a part of life that even Jesus experienced. The shortest verse in the Bible is John 11:35, and it says, "Jesus wept."

Ecclesiastes says that crying is a part of the cycle of life: "[There is] a time to weep, and a time to laugh; a time to mourn, and a time to dance" (Ecclesiastes 3:4). And in Romans 12:15, we are commanded to cry: "Rejoice with those who rejoice, weep with those who weep."

The first words of Jesus after he rose from the dead were said to a woman. Jesus said, "Woman, why are you weeping? Whom are you seeking?" (John 20:15). Jesus knew the answer, and he was there to reassure her. His presence helped her know that everything was going to be okay and that she did not need to cry anymore.

One of the most comforting verses in Scripture is found in Revelation when it speaks of heaven. It says, "He will wipe every tear from their eyes. There will be no more death or mourning or crying or pain, for the old order of things has passed away" (Revelation 21:4 NIV). In heaven, our tears will be over forever! And if we return to the writings of David, we see in Psalm 56 he says, "When I am afraid, I put my trust in you. In God, whose word I praise, in God I trust; I shall not be afraid" (vv. 3–4).

Notice how David went from being afraid to declaring, "I will not be afraid!" What settled his anxious thoughts? Putting his trust in God.

Is there something keeping you up at night? Trust God.

Is there something that is causing you to give way to fear? Trust God.

Push out the darkness.

Stand in the light.

I know that sometimes it doesn't feel like God is for us. Just like when I was a kid, and my parents would tell me to do things I did not want to do, I could not see then how much my parents were for me. But now, looking back, I can see clearly. I was loved.

You may not be able to see the big picture right now, but you can trust God and release whatever burdens you are carrying to him. He loves you.

Sit in the Light

This past summer my son was selling some of his Nike Air Jordan shoes on eBay. He pulled out the pair from the back of the closet and brought them to me. I remembered those old shoes. He'd gotten them as a gift in junior high, and what made them special was that they glowed in the dark. I remembered when he'd worn them to the movie theater with friends and then came home so excited because they had glowed all throughout the movie. He'd found that hilarious.

Those old shoes had sat in the dark closet for years, and now they had no glow left in them, so he wondered if they were worth much anymore. Then I reminded him that all he needed to do was set them outside in the sun for a few hours, and they would glow again. So out he went to the back deck with his shoes, and just a few hours later my son found the darkest room in the house to test the shoes. Sure enough, just a few hours in the sunlight and they were glowing bright as could be.

Friend, when we sit in the darkness of life's struggles and pain, we grow dim. The darkness enfolds us, and any light we once had is snuffed out. But Psalm 119:105 tells us that God's Word is a lamp to our feet and a light for our path. When we live in the light of God's Word, his light shines into the darkness and we begin to see clearly again.

Change Your Prayers

Every day we tap on a screen with our finger or tap on a mouse to click. We tap, and the response is quick. Over and over, we tap and repeat the quick response. When we tap and the response is slow, we get frustrated. We check our settings and check our Wi-Fi signal. We try again and tap again. If we get no response, we know that something is not right.

Our relationship with God can feel like this. Sometimes we pray and it feels like nothing happened. So we pray again, and we wait. Then we pray again, and we wait . . . and wait . . . and wait. In our waiting, we can become frustrated with God's silence. We are not accustomed to slow responses in our culture. But God works differently than our fast-paced, fast-food, fast-speed internet world.

It takes effort to walk with the Lord daily because, let's be real, sometimes praying the same thing day in and day out can get boring. If you are praying the same things over and over—like praying for your family, friends, finances, the church, and people's crises, it can get repetitive.

So it's time to switch it up!

Pray the Bible

This one change will change your prayer life dramatically. Take a verse or passage of Scripture from Psalms, Proverbs, or the

New Testament and personalize it. Pray the verses over your own life and over your loved ones' lives.

Let Scripture shape your prayers.

When my children were little, an older woman in my church shared how she prays the Proverbs over her children every day. She showed me how she had taken a photo album and turned it into her prayer journal. She used index cards and wrote verses on them and then slipped the cards into the pockets of the photo album. Then during her prayer time, she would flip through her album and pray those verses over her children.

So, I began to follow her example. I created an album and used that for a while, but eventually I found myself doing my daily reading in Scripture and then pausing and praying what I just read over my life and the lives of my loved ones.

For years, I have read a chapter of Proverbs a day using the chapter that corresponds with the date. So, on the first of the month, I read Proverbs 1, on the second of the month I read Proverbs 2, and so on. As I read through Proverbs, I pick out one of the verses from that chapter, and that is the one that I pray over my life and my children's lives. I also love to do this from the book of Psalms.

Let Me Show You How This Is Done

Look at Psalm 40, verse 1, which says, "I waited patiently for the Lord." Now, if you have children, pray this over your children: "Lord, please help my children to wait patiently for you." Pray this over your friends: "Lord, please strengthen my friends in their waiting." Pray this over your own life: "Lord, give me the patience I need to wait on you."

Then move on to the next line. Pray God's Word line by line over your own life and over your loved ones, and if a verse does not apply, skip it. You can do this using verses from Paul's letters in the New Testament as well.

Declare the Promises of God's Word

As we let the light of God's Word shine into our lives, it is powerful! You see, the darkness cannot overcome the light. It must flee when the light shines into the darkness: "The light shines in the darkness, and the darkness has not overcome it" (John 1:5 NIV).

We must stand firm on the promises of God's Word. As you read the Word and pray the Word, write down any promises you see in the Word. God says he will never leave you nor forsake you. God says you are loved. God says you are forgiven. God says you are wonderfully made.

Declare these promises over your life, and remind others as well. Not only do we need the light of God's Word in our lives, but so many around us are trapped in darkness as well. Once we experience the freedom that only God can give, God wants to use us to free others. We become the light in their lives that they need.

Ask the Holy Spirit for Help

Remember this when you don't know how to pray: the Holy Spirit is with you. Ask the Holy Spirit to help you pray. Look at what Romans 8:26–27 (NIV) says:

> In the same way, the Spirit helps us in our weakness. We do not know what we ought to pray for, but the Spirit himself intercedes for us through wordless groans. And he who searches our hearts knows the mind of the Spirit, because the Spirit intercedes for God's people in accordance with the will of God."

Be Still

When you still feel defeated after praying God's Word and declaring God's promises, be still. Be silent, and ask the Holy

Spirit to intercede for you. Some of my deepest prayers have had no words at all. I have sat in my tears and simply said to God, "I have no words." I knew that he knew exactly what I was thinking and feeling, and so I said no words at all. In my pain and sorrow, I would pray, "Please, Lord, just help me. Just for today, give me the strength I need."

God loves you. He is with you and for you. He wants to hear from you. So let's practice this one change this week. When you pray, open your Bible and pray Scripture, and then go forward standing firm in the light of God's truth.

REFLECTION QUESTIONS

1. What is something you have been praying for a very long time? How can you guard yourself from the lie of the enemy that tempts you to believe that God is not listening?

2. Read Psalm 56:8–9. How does it comfort you to know that God does in fact see every tear that falls on your pillow, and he is surely for you?

3. Praying God's Word is a powerful way to change your prayer life. Have you ever used this method of prayer? How could you implement this more in your life?

4. Let's practice this method of prayer right now using Psalm 56:8–9. You could pray something like this: "Lord, I know you keep count of my tossing and turning at night. Your Word says you see my tears. Help me when I am weak to keep trusting in you and believing you are for me." Now go back to Psalm 56:3–4 and pray these verses over your life as well.

5. Romans 8:26–27 tells us we can pray without words and let the Holy Spirit intercede for us. Do you ever pray in this way? Why or why not? When you are overwhelmed with emotion, how would remembering to be still and silent in prayer help you?

3 How Can Someone I Can't See Help Me?

I was in a hurry with more things on my to-do list than I could ever get done in a day. This had become my new normal since becoming a single mom. I always felt a step behind. So it was another day, like many others, where I was rushing around trying to get things done, and I needed to do a quick stop at the grocery store. It was about ten degrees out, and my car had not warmed up between home and the grocery store. I quickly parked my car, ran into the store, picked up a few items, did the self-checkout, and was back to my car in record time.

Then I pushed the button to start my car, and nothing happened. I tried again. The car made a weird sound, and then nothing again. I looked up, and there was a woman staring at me from inside her car, parked facing me. That felt awkward. So I quickly looked down and began scrolling on my phone, thinking of who would be available to call for help, while also thinking I would try to start the car again once this woman wasn't staring at me.

I was annoyed. I did not have time for this, plus I hate asking people for help. I like to be self-sufficient, but I had made the mistake of not keeping jumper cables in my car. This meant I was going to have to ask someone in this parking lot for help or call someone.

I glanced up, and the lady was still looking at me through her oversized glasses. Again, it felt awkward. She got out of her very old Volkswagen bug, slung her long black braid over her shoulder, and popped her car's hood. Then she walked over to me, and I sheepishly opened my door.

It was freezing outside, and all she had on was an oversized jean jacket with patches. She kindly asked if I needed help, and I admitted that I did. Then she explained that her car was dead too. Well, that was an unexpected twist! We both had dead cars. Now what were we going to do?

This day was turning from bad to worse very quickly, and I am sure it showed all over my face. But then she went on to explain that her car battery died all the time when the weather was this cold, and so she came prepared. She said as soon as she got her car going, she would jump mine.

I am sure I looked confused, but before I got a word out, she explained that she had a battery-charged jump starter that she carried with her all the time. She turned around, went to her trunk, pulled out her little charger, and while she put the clips on her battery, she explained how she had gotten a great deal on the charger. Normally they were two hundred dollars, but she had gotten it on sale for just sixty dollars and was so grateful.

Within two minutes her car was running. Now it was my turn. "Pop the hood," she said. Hmmmm, pop the hood. *Oh goodness, Courtney, this is not the time for a brain freeze.* I had opened my hood before to put both oil and windshield wiper fluid in, but for the life of me, I could not find the latch inside the car.

She was a patient woman. She came over, pulled the latch inside, then pulled the latch outside, and quickly the hood was up and her jump starter was on my battery. I was in my car when she said, "Okay, start her up!"

I pushed the button, and my car started right away. I paused. A thank-you didn't feel like enough. Clearly her car was very old and she did not have the money for a new battery. I dug in my purse for as much cash as I could find and then got out of the car and handed it to her. Her jaw could have hit the ground. She said no. I said yes, please take it, and I leaned in for a hug. She hugged me back and said a sincere thank-you, and then I quickly left.

God Uses People

We are the hands and feet of Jesus. God wants to use us to help others. But sometimes as believers, we can say insensitive things to people who are going through hard times.

"God never gives you more than you can handle."

"Everything happens for a reason."

"Worrying is a sin. Don't worry, God will provide."

"God uses suffering to sanctify us. Suffer well."

Some of these are true, and we mean well when we say them to others, but they don't help. You know what helps? Someone showing up. How do I know this to be true? Because God has used people over and over in my life to show up and help me. This is how God works. He uses people. We are his hands and feet.

God knew that day when I ran to the grocery store that my car battery would die, and in his sovereignty, he provided this woman, who just happened to have a charger, to help me.

I stand in awe of our God.

His word is true. He does provide in more ways than one. He is *for* me.

Remember the Birds

> Look at the birds of the air; they do not sow or reap or store away in barns, and yet your heavenly Father feeds them. Are you not much more valuable than they? Can any one of you by worrying add a single hour to your life?
>
> Matthew 6:26–27 NIV

Remember that verse? As a single mom, I may have been a little more needy than the average woman. Every single time something broke in my home or on my car it felt like a crisis. It was annoying, but each time I was reminded to look at the birds. We are much more valuable than they are to God.

God Cares

Well, I know God cares, but there have been times when I've thought, *How can someone I can't see help me?* I regularly get on my knees in prayer, but when I'm done praying, I'm still all alone. I still have the problem before me that I must figure out. I know I'm supposed to leave my burdens with Jesus, but some crises must be dealt with immediately, and it's on me to deal with them.

I regularly feel like I'm playing a game of tag where I am always *It*. There are days that I just wish God would come in the flesh and help me. Then I am reminded that he has shown up in more ways than I could ever count through family, friends, strangers, and yes, even YouTube. YouTube has solved many problems over the years. Strangers on YouTube have taught me many things, like how to unclog my garbage disposal, how to teach my kids maneuverability for their driver's license tests, how to tie my son's tie and teach him to shave, how to light a pilot light on a water heater, and more!

As I look back over my life, it's interesting for me to note that God does not always use the same people to help me. I am so grateful for the help that my family and friends have given me over the years. They are all a great blessing to me. But often it's been strangers like the lady in the parking lot that day. I have had similar scenarios in home maintenance stores like Home Depot. I've been lost in the store, trying to find what I need to fix something in my home, and another shopper will ask if I need help, and by the time I'm leaving, I not only have what I need to fix my problem but have full instructions as well.

When I consider how God has used people like this in my life, I'm reminded that I need to be that person for others. We can be the one who shows up in the lives of others. God wants to use you and me to be the hands and feet of Jesus in the lives of our family, friends, *and* complete strangers.

God Is Always with You

It is not always physical help that we need. We need spiritual support as well, and we should not try to use physical things to solve spiritual problems. Remembering that God is always with us reassures us that we are never alone, even when we feel lonely.

My eighteen-year-old daughter has an Echo. An Echo is an interactive speaker. You can speak to it and tell it to do things for you. For example my daughter will say, "Echo, play worship music." And like a radio, it will play music for her. Or she will say, "Echo, wake me up at 6:00 a.m. tomorrow." And the next morning at 6:00 a.m. an alarm will automatically go off.

Most nights, I sit on her bed, and we chat about life as she falls asleep. Every now and then, while we are talking, the Echo will light up and start to talk to us. It is a little disturbing, and it is uncomfortable to think that it is listening to everything we say!

Have you ever been in a store and you noticed cameras watching you? Even if you are doing nothing wrong, it just feels strange and a little uncomfortable.

Then there's baby monitors. I used to love to listen to my babies in their cribs through the monitor. When they woke up from their nap, I enjoyed listening to their cooing and jibber jabber. The baby monitor was in their rooms because I loved them and wanted to be sure I could take good care of my babies. In the same way, God loves us, he is always listening, and he is always taking care of us.

So when we think about God's presence always being with us, it should not be disturbing or uncomfortable but rather a comfort to us. But sometimes we'd rather God be distant. Like the Echo or the cameras in stores, it might feel uncomfortable to think about how God is always watching us. But we cannot hide from God. He intimately knows us, and this is a good thing!

Ten Ways God Intimately Knows You

David wrote a beautiful song in Psalm 139. This psalm focuses on the omniscience of God and God's ability to see and know all about us. Let's look at Psalm 139 together and see what God sees.

1) *God knows your habits.*

> O Lord, you have searched me and known me!
> You know when I sit down and when I rise up;
>
> Psalm 139:1–2

God understands your life. He is totally familiar with your habits. He knows when you sit down and when you stand up.

2) *God knows your thoughts.*

> You discern my thoughts from afar.
>
> Psalm 139:2

Even if you don't say a word, God knows what you are thinking. He knows your good thoughts and the bad ones. He knows your personality, emotions, strengths, and weaknesses. Nothing is hidden from God.

3) ***God knows your location.***

> You search out my path and my lying down
> and are acquainted with all my ways.
>
> Psalm 139:3

God is like a GPS. He knows your location. He knows when you are gone from home and driving somewhere, and he knows when you are home and asleep. He is acquainted with all your ways.

4) ***God knows your words.***

> Even before a word is on my tongue,
> behold, O Lord, you know it altogether.
>
> Psalm 139:4

God knows what you are going to say before you even say it. He knows the intent of your heart. Consider, if God walked into the room today, would you change the way you talk? God is always in the room with you.

5) ***God knows your past, present, and future.***

> You hem me in, behind and before,
> and lay your hand upon me.
>
> Psalm 139:5

God goes behind you. He knows your past. God goes before you. He knows your future. And his hand is upon you now. He is with you in the present. God is always with us, guarding us and protecting us. We can rest easy at night knowing that our future is in God's hands.

At this point in the psalm, David pauses and stands in awe of God.

> Such knowledge is too wonderful for me;
> it is high; I cannot attain it.
>
> Where shall I go from your Spirit?
> Or where shall I flee from your presence?
> If I ascend to heaven, you are there!
> If I make my bed in Sheol, you are there!
> If I take the wings of the morning
> and dwell in the uttermost parts of the sea,
> even there your hand shall lead me,
> and your right hand shall hold me.
>
> Psalm 139:6–10

Let's pause midway and just ponder the awesomeness of our God that we see in Psalm 139.

Our God is omniscient.
He knows all.
Our God is omnipresent.
He is in all places at once.
He doesn't just know everything—
he knows you.
And he isn't just everywhere—
he is with you.
Our God is an *awesome* God!

Okay, back to his Word.

6) ***God sees you in the darkness.***

> If I say, "Surely the darkness shall cover me,
> and the light about me be night,"
> even the darkness is not dark to you;

the night is bright as the day,
for darkness is as light with you.

Psalm 139:11–12

When we feel swallowed up in the darkness of our difficult circumstances and we can't see what's ahead, God sees. The night is as day to him because he sees all. He is not distant. There are no secrets with God.

7) ***God knows your DNA.***

For you formed my inward parts;
you knitted me together in my mother's womb.
I praise you, for I am fearfully and wonderfully made.
Wonderful are your works;
my soul knows it very well.
My frame was not hidden from you,
when I was being made in secret,
intricately woven in the depths of the earth.

Psalm 139:13–15

God is self-existent, and he is not just the creator of the world, he created you! He created you in your mother's womb, and you are amazing. Your body is unique, complex, and intricate, and it points to an intelligent designer who loves you.

8) ***God knows the number of your days.***

Your eyes saw my unformed substance;
in your book were written, every one of them,
the days that were formed for me,
when as yet there was none of them.

Psalm 139:16

In the NIV this verse reads like this: "Your eyes saw my unformed body; all the days ordained for me were written in your book before one of them came to be."

God is all-knowing. He knows how and when you will die before you are even born. One hundred percent of us will die, and we will all stand face-to-face with the all-knowing God. We will give an account for how we lived; therefore, we should live each day for him, until we see him face-to-face.

9) ***God is always thinking of you.***

> How precious to me are your thoughts, O God!
> How vast is the sum of them!
> If I would count them, they are more than the sand.
> I awake, and I am still with you.
>
> Psalm 139:17–18

God's thoughts of you are immeasurable. They are precious. They are vast, and they are more numerous than the grains of sand. Have you ever tried to count grains of sand? It's not possible. You are on God's mind a lot!

10) ***God knows your heart.***

> Search me, O God, and know my heart!
> Try me and know my thoughts!
> And see if there be any grievous way in me,
> and lead me in the way everlasting!
>
> Psalm 139:23–24

God knows the depths of your heart and mind. He knows all of your emotions, desires, motives, and intentions. He has a deep understanding of who you are and knows your innermost thoughts and anxieties.

In conclusion, the psalmist asks God to lead him in the way everlasting. Our most vital need is our need for a savior. While we were sinners, Christ died for us. You were on God's mind before you were born, and Jesus loves you so much, he died on the cross for your sins. He wants a relationship with you. If you have not accepted Jesus as your personal Savior, what are you waiting for? You are so loved! Just pray and confess your sins and place your faith in Jesus today.

If you are born again, do not let darkness and doubt take over your thoughts. It is easy to wonder where God is in the midst of our mess. The enemy wants you to feel alone but you can be assured, God is with you! He knows you intimately and loves you deeply. His presence and truth push out the darkness. Stand in the light, and take it just one day at a time.

REFLECTION QUESTIONS

1. God uses people to help us. Has a stranger ever helped you? Think back to a time when God used a friend or stranger to help. How were they God's hands and feet to you?

2. God wants to use you! Is there someone in your life right now who needs help? How can you be used by God in their situation? If not, I challenge you to keep your eyes open when you are out this week and watch for ways that you can be a blessing to someone else in need.

3. How does it make you feel to know that God knows your every thought, all your habits, your words, your past, your present, and your future? Does it scare you or make you feel more loved?

4. Look at Psalm 139:17–18. What does David compare God's thoughts to? Have you ever been to the beach and had sand stuck all over your feet, towel, and in your beach bag? How many grains would you say were stuck

all over your things? Now imagine how many more grains of sand are on every beach. How do these compare to the number of God's thoughts of you?

5. As sinners, our greatest need is salvation. How did God show up for you in the flesh when he died on the cross? Give him thanks and praise him today for his work in your life.

4 | Why Is Being Still Not Working?

I homeschooled my children for seven years. During the separation from their dad, my kids began attending a Christian school a few districts away. Every morning I drove my kids to the local elementary school, and there they got on a bus with other kids headed to the same school. We usually had to wait in the car for about five minutes for the bus to arrive, so while we were waiting, I always prayed with them. Eventually, I started reading a passage of Scripture with them as well.

The chapter I chose to read over and over to them was Psalm 46. It is one of my favorite chapters in the Bible. These are the words I read to them daily:

> God is our refuge and strength,
> a very present help in trouble.
> Therefore we will not fear though the earth gives way,
> though the mountains be moved into the heart of the sea,
> though its waters roar and foam,
> though the mountains tremble at its swelling. *Selah*
>
> Psalm 46:1–3

God Is Our Safe Place

During this time, my children's entire world was being shaken. Their dad was gone in another state, and the homeschool life they were accustomed to had come to an end. They were making new friends and learning to be responsible for themselves away from me and each other, while wondering what was happening at home. Would we have to sell our house and move? Would their dad change his mind and come home? Was their mom going to be okay?

Our world had been rocked, and we were scared. When an animal is scared it runs to its hole to find refuge. Psalm 46:1 tells us that "God is our refuge and strength, a very present help in trouble."

God is our safe place. And since God is our safe place, we can have no fear, even when the worst disasters hit and our world is shaken. The psalmist says, "*Selah*."

In the Hebrew, the word *Selah* means "pause."[1] Stop the fear. Be still.

Be Still

I also loved reading these powerful words from the end of Psalm 46 to the kids:

> "Be still, and know that I am God.
> I will be exalted among the nations,
> I will be exalted in the earth!"
> The Lord of hosts is with us;
> the God of Jacob is our fortress. *Selah*
>
> Psalm 46:10–11

Be still.

Oh, how I wanted my kids to trust in God and know that he is above all kings and kingdoms. He is mighty and powerful.

The Lord of heavenly hosts of angels is with us! When we pause and reflect and consider how great our God is, we can rest in him and be still.

Selah.

But What if Being Still Isn't Working?

One day after the divorce was final, I received a gift from a friend. The gift included wall art with the words *Be Still* printed on it. I knew just where this print needed to go. I walked over to the collage of photos on my living room wall and took down our family photo. With tears streaming down my face, I looked at our sweet family on the beach. I paused and remembered the fun we had on our last summer vacation before our world fell apart. The kids were so little, and we all looked so happy. The pain was too much to bear. After opening the frame, I took the words *Be Still* and laid the art directly over the photo of our little family of four. With a heavy heart, I slowly closed the frame back up and hung it back on the wall.

Covering the family photo was painful, but it needed to be done. It hurt to cover it up, but it hurt even more to look at that picture daily. To this day, that wall art is still hanging on my wall in the same place, and I doubt anyone knows what's tucked behind those words except me. I know. And I also know that God wanted me to be still and trust him with all the pain and sorrow I was wrestling with.

Wrestling with God

God says to be still, but what if being still isn't working?

Since receiving the *Be Still* wall art, I've noticed that there's a lot of Christian merchandise items with the words *Be Still* on them. I had a friend tell me once that she prefers to keep busy, because when she is still, she thinks too much, and when she thinks too much, her anxiety really gets the best of her.

What if in your stillness all the emotions you have pushed down begin to bubble up under the surface? What if you are overcome with anger, bitterness, sadness, grief, and anxiety? In the coming chapters, we are going to address all these emotions because it's important that we deal with them biblically. It is not healthy to shove them down and not deal with them.

But maybe you are like me and you do trust God and you do feel like you can be still and rest in him, but sometimes you feel like God might be holding out on you. We look at other people's lives and we compare our lives to theirs and we think, *Hmm—why do they seem to have less trouble than I have?* And then instead of delighting in the good gifts God has given us, we pull back a little from God because we aren't sure we can completely trust him.

I remember in the past, every spring my air conditioner would freeze up, and so I would have to pay a couple hundred dollars for the repair man to come out and fix it. Eventually, after a few years in a row of this, I decided to splurge and get a whole new air conditioner so I would not keep losing money fixing the old one. The same thing was also happening with my car. One little thing after another kept needing to be fixed, and eventually I decided to get a new car so I could stop dealing with car repairs.

I was tired of things breaking, so I thought I had fixed my problem by buying new things. Only life does not work that way. It just doesn't cooperate! As soon as one problem was solved, I had a new problem. First it was a broken toilet, followed by a broken dishwasher. Right now, my trampoline has a tear from one side to the other. Luckily my kids weren't hurt when they fell through, but it feels like it is always something. And I have had moments when I have said to the Lord in desperation, "Please, not today!"

But then there are other days when I am discouraged with unanswered prayers, and then suddenly there's this shift—God answers my prayer in a way I did not expect. And right before my eyes, life is unfolding and prayers are being answered and my heart is filled with joy.

And though some of my biggest life prayers have not been answered, a whole bunch of little prayers under the umbrella of the big prayers are being answered. There are also things I have never asked God for or even thought to ask God for that have unexpectedly come into my life, and I see the good hand of God watching over me.

For example, I mentioned the trampoline splitting down the middle. The day my daughter and her friend were jumping, I wasn't praying for their protection. I wasn't worried that the trampoline would tear, but it did, and God was near, and they were fine when they hit the ground. I thank God that even when I wasn't praying for their safety, he was protecting them.

And so we do not need to be suspicious that maybe God is holding out on us. We can be still and trust in him. He is with us, and he loves us.

Selah.

Is It Wrong to Wrestle with God?

There are so many strong women of faith in my church. They seem to breeze right through life's struggles and never wrestle with God. If they do wrestle with God, they don't speak of it.

So, what if in your stillness you begin to wrestle with God?

Is it wrong to wrestle with God?

In the book of Genesis, Jacob wrestled with God. Jacob, who had stolen from his brother, Esau, was scared to return to his hometown, where Esau was angry with him. As he lay wide awake in fear, he began to wrestle with God.

> And Jacob was left alone. And a man wrestled with him until the breaking of the day. When the man saw that he did not prevail against Jacob, he touched his hip socket, and Jacob's hip was put out of joint as he wrestled with him. Then he said, "Let me go, for the day has broken." But Jacob said, "I will not let you go unless you bless me." And he said to him, "What is your name?" And he said, "Jacob." Then he said, "Your name shall no longer be called Jacob, but Israel, for you have striven with God and with men, and have prevailed."
>
> Genesis 32:24–28

Jacob wrestled with God!

He wanted comfort from God, and it came in the form of a wrestling match. While Jacob wrestled with God, God touched Jacob's hip and put it out of joint. This did not stop Jacob from wrestling. Jacob clung to God with all his might and begged him for a blessing. After Jacob's wrestling match was over, Jacob limped the rest of his life.

Wrestling with God Changes Us

When Jacob was done wrestling with God, he had a new name and a new identity. God changed his name from Jacob to Israel.

Friends, after we wrestle with God, we are changed. While we are wrestling, God does not always give us answers—instead he gives us more of himself. This develops a deeper intimacy with God, because after we have wrestled a bit, we will find comfort, our faith will be increased, and we will be changed because of our intimate encounter with our Heavenly Father.

Sometimes I think we don't wrestle with God enough.

Rather than digging in deep and lingering long in his Word and laying out our soul in prayer, we turn to worldly

Band-Aids to solve our problems. What if we got away from our family and friends, closed our devotional books, shut down our phones, and we got alone and simply wrestled it out with God?

No quick, easy fixes—just you and God for hours.

We Google and click and scroll and click and meet in coffee houses in search of answers. We buy book after book and watch movie after movie to escape our troubles. We plan far-off travels to get away from it all, but our baggage inside our souls goes with us. Don't get me wrong, God gave us many good things to enjoy, but if we are not careful, these things will become poor substitutes for intimacy with God.

When God invited Jacob into a wrestling match, Jacob was filled with anxiety and completely caught up in his mess. Once Jacob began wrestling, there was no more room for his anxiety.

His focus was one-hundred-percent on God.

I have learned from my own wrestling matches that God does not show up the way I necessarily want him to. Like a toddler stomping her feet, I want God to give me what I ask for, when I ask for it.

Instead, God knows my deeper needs. He knows I need to completely focus on him. He knows I need comfort. He knows I need increased faith. He knows I need to depend on him alone. He knows I need to be changed and that I need more of him.

Selah.

Be still.

God is with you, and he loves you. Whatever is burdening you today, take it to the Lord. God is not afraid of the darkness. Invite him in, and wrestle out with him your fear and discouragement. And always remember, when you are wrestling with God, the darkness cannot win! "The light shines in the darkness, and the darkness has not overcome it" (John 1:5 NIV).

REFLECTION QUESTIONS

1. What happens when you are still? Are you filled with negative emotions, or are you at peace?

2. When life is chaotic and hard, who or what do you tend to turn to first? Look at Psalm 46:1. God is not distant. How does remembering the nearness of God as a refuge and strength calm your fears?

3. God speaks in Psalm 46:10, and he says to be still and know that he is God. The stillness he speaks of is not one of just sitting still but rather being still in our souls. How does knowing he is God still your anxious soul?

4. Jacob grew closer to God through wrestling with him. His wrestling match led to resting. Have you experienced this? When was the last time you wrestled with God and found peace on the other side?

5. Is there an area in your life where you are wrestling with God right now? God initiated his wrestling match with Jacob. Do you think God may be inviting you in deeper with him? Go into his presence in prayer and his Word, and don't be afraid to wrestle it out so you can truly be at rest.

5 Do All Things Really Work Together for Good?

One of the most quoted verses from the New Testament is Romans 8:28: "And we know that for those who love God all things work together for good, for those who are called according to his purpose." God says that for those who love him, everything that comes into our lives is working together for good. But how can this be true? Cancer is not good. The loss of a child is not good. Divorce is not good. War is not good. Sickness is not good. Dashed hopes and dreams are not good.

There's a dichotomy between knowing that God is good and knowing that bad things in our lives are not good. And that is the very reason God gave us this verse. Because he knows that the greatest good for us is that we trust him when things are not good. God has a master plan, and he is at work in a thousand different ways that we cannot see.

God Is Faithful, But Our Emotions Often Tell Us Otherwise

I remember talking to a friend before my divorce was finalized, and she told me that one day she believed God would use what I was going through to minister to women who were also going through divorce. I immediately bristled. No. No. No. How could she even say such a thing? That was not the ministry I wanted. I did not want a divorce, and I did not want a ministry for women going through divorce. I adamantly wanted reconciliation. I wanted to be married. Period. End of story.

Looking back, she saw clearly the good that God could bring from my horrible situation. She knew that if I walked through this dark valley and persevered in faith, on the other side, God could use this for my good and his glory. But at the time, my emotions were telling me otherwise. I could not see or even imagine anything good coming from what I was going through.

I was flooded with fear, sadness, and all sorts of emotions, and so Romans 8:28 fell very flat for me. In the next section, we are going to look at specific emotions that the enemy uses to put us in a headlock and convince us that God doesn't work all things together for good. The enemy's lies can hold us in darkness.

You see, God made us with emotions, and emotions are powerful. We can experience very high highs and very low lows and everything in between. As a matter of fact, if we try to suppress them, we will have trouble, but on the opposite extreme, if we let them control us, we will also have trouble.

Are you an emotional person?

King David, one of the writers of the book of Psalms, was very emotional. Psalms is filled with feelings we all experience, including love, joy, peace, sadness, pain, suffering, anger, fear, doubt, and more. If you've felt it, Psalms expresses it. It is a wonderful book of the Bible to read daily for encouragement, comfort, and guidance when you feel overwhelmed. What I love most about the book of Psalms is how David expressed deep and sincere faith amid all his emotions.

Sometimes Our Feelings Are Liars

Whatever we think about most grows. So if we allow our emotions to dominate us and we don't run them through the filter of God's Word, we put ourselves in danger of being lied to by the enemy. When we believe his lies, it can lead to us doubting if God is really working all things together for good.

Jesus tells us in John 8:44:

> He [the devil] was a murderer from the beginning, and does not stand in the truth, because there is no truth in him. When he lies, he speaks out of his own character, for he is a liar and the father of lies.

The enemy is a liar. He cannot create thoughts in your mind, but he can lie to you. And that is just what he does! He wants to murder you, only he does not use a knife or gun to do it—he uses lies.

Jesus said the devil was a murderer from the beginning. He is referring to Adam and Eve in the garden of Eden. The serpent lied to them, and they believed his lie over the truth of what God had told them. This led to death and the fall of all humankind.

Oh, friend, what lies are you being bombarded with right now? Do you have thoughts that come from past pain and wounds in your life that play on repeat? Do you have fears that creep up on you and keep you up at night? Do you have anger, sadness, or insecurities that you just can't seem to shake?

Maybe you don't even know what feelings and emotions are lying to you. You might feel emotionally off but are not able to put a finger on what is getting you down. Maybe you prefer to hide your wounds and be strong so that no one knows you are hurting, but pretending does not set you free.

We all know thoughts are not harmless because our body recognizes wrong thoughts. Have you ever been highly stressed or worried, and you literally got sick to your stomach or got a terrible headache? Your body knows when you are entertaining lies and hurtful thoughts. So you can act strong or hide it from others, but your body still knows. Harmful emotions need to be addressed.

The Enemy Wants You Isolated

When we hide, we get isolated. God gave us the church for a reason. God knows that we need to live in community with other believers. Isolated people can become sick emotionally and spiritually. Our minds get assaulted with the lies from the enemy with no outlet for our thoughts to be discussed and no inlet for wisdom and godly thoughts to come in. This closed circuit lends to a murky mind.

It's the difference between a beautiful river that has water flowing along and a swamp that has no outlet. The mind of a person who is isolated can become like a swamp. Satan gets us cornered and overcomes us with feelings and emotions that are full of lies.

Emotions and Feelings Are Not Permanent

We do not have to stay stuck in the swamp of lies permanently. Jesus came that we might be free. His truth sets us free from the bondage of the lies of the enemy. The good news is, we can change our thinking, and by changing our thinking, our feelings and emotions are changed. And once we are set free, we can help set others free as well!

What we need is God's truth, and his truth is found in his Word. God's Word is vital to changing us. It brings light to the darkness and dispels the lies of the enemy.

First Thessalonians 5:16–18 gives us a mindset for living well: "Rejoice always, pray without ceasing, give thanks in all circumstances; for this is the will of God in Christ Jesus for you." Do you sometimes wonder what God's will is for you? This verse tells us. It says his will is that we would always be rejoicing, praying, and giving thanks. Rejoicing, praying, and giving thanks all start in the mind. They are powerful practices that change our thinking.

Paul in Philippians 4:8 gives us a list of ways to filter our thoughts:

> Finally, brothers, whatever is true,
> whatever is honorable,
> whatever is just,
> whatever is pure,
> whatever is lovely,
> whatever is commendable,
> if there is any excellence,
> if there is anything worthy of praise,
> think about these things.

Every time I change my furnace filter, it is full of dirt and dust. If I wait too long to change the filter, it goes from dark gray to black. It is clearly working to catch all the impurities in the air from flowing into my home.

In the same way, Philippians 4:8 is a great verse to use to filter our thoughts. We need to be asking ourselves regularly if the thoughts we are having are true, honorable, just, pure, lovely, commendable, and excellent. If not, we need to catch those negative thoughts at the door of our minds and stop them before they alter our emotions in unhealthy ways.

We do have a choice in the matter. We do not have to live surrendered to the lies of the enemy. You see, once we are aware—like we are right now—and we live intentionally, our thought patterns that seemed to have power over us are weakened. And as they are weakened, the stronghold of the enemy begins to break down, and we begin to experience victory over the darkness in our lives.

To live victorious does not mean we win a final battle against the enemy and then he is gone forever. As long as we are alive, we are going to be in this battle between light and darkness. And so winning for us is being aware of the enemy's schemes and speaking truth out loud when we are attacked. It is staying in the fight and persevering when we are tired, and it is being able to say with Paul at the end of our lives, "I have fought the good fight, I have finished the race, I have kept the faith" (2 Timothy 4:7).

There are times the enemy has stolen my peace, stolen my joy, stolen my self-worth, and caused me to be in despair, but by the grace of God, I'm still standing, and I will not give up until I have finished my race.

Friend, keep the faith!

All Things Do Work Together for Good

And so that brings us back to Romans 8:28. God's Word says that he is working all things together for good in our lives. Oh, I know how hard it is to believe this at times, but we must trust God that *all* means *all*. This is true even when our feelings tell us otherwise.

God is for us. Look at how Romans 8 ends, where Paul writes this:

> What then shall we say to these things? If God is for us, who can be against us? . . . Who shall separate us from the love of Christ? Shall tribulation, or distress, or persecution, or famine, or nakedness, or danger, or sword? As it is written,"For your sake we are being killed all the day long; we are regarded as sheep to be slaughtered." No, in all these things we are more than conquerors through him who loved us. For I am sure that neither death nor life, nor angels nor rulers, nor things present

> nor things to come, nor powers, nor height nor depth, nor anything else in all creation, will be able to separate us from the love of God in Christ Jesus our Lord.
>
> Romans 8:31, 35–39

Paul listed the many troubles he had faced, yet he had overcome them all. Friend, when life is overwhelming and you feel like the enemy is pulling you into darkness, you do not have to give in to the enemy.

You are a child of God! Hold on to the hope of eternal life. Walk in the light. Be aware that Satan will try to draw you away from the light, and always remember, "Greater is He who is in you than he who is in the world" (1 John 4:4 NASB). Do not fall for the devil's schemes.

Fight back!

Fight back on your knees in prayer.

Fight back with truth by memorizing and meditating on Scripture daily.

Fight back by putting on some worship music and singing your heart out to God.

Fight back by grabbing a notebook and listing the things you are grateful for daily.

Fight back, because we do not just win in the end, we are meant to be winning right now.

"We are more than conquerors" (Romans 8:37)—*are* is in present tense. That means we are conquerors right now. Actually, the text says we are *more* than conquerors. This means we aren't just winning by a little bit; we are winning by a lot.

Trust God.

Nothing can come your way that is not working out in the end for your good and his glory. So as you face the mountaintops and valleys of your daily life, stand firm in your faith. You can be certain and live confident that he has a good plan for you. Keep walking with the King.

REFLECTION QUESTIONS

1. Romans 8:28 says that "for those who love God all things work together for good." Tell of a time when something not good in your life worked out to be good for you. How does remembering how God worked in your life encourage you as you face some of the hard things in your life right now?

2. John 8:44 says the devil is "the father of lies." What lies are you being bombarded with right now? Are there any negative emotions like anger, fear, or insecurity that play on repeat in your mind?

3. Use Philippians 4:8 as a filter for your emotions and thoughts. Run the lies you wrote down from the previous question through the list of things we are to be thinking about as believers. Are they true, honorable, just, pure, lovely, commendable, or excellent? If not, you must get rid of these thoughts!

4. According to 1 Thessalonians 5:16–18, what is God's will for you? How does obeying God's Word and practicing these things in your life help rid your mind of negative thought patterns?

5. You are meant to be more than a conqueror. How can you use prayer, Scripture, worship, or a gratitude list to be more intentional this week with fighting the lies of the enemy?

PART 2

OVERCOMING THE DARKNESS

1 You have searched me, LORD,
  and you know me.
2 You know when I sit and when I rise;
  you perceive my thoughts from afar.
3 You discern my going out and my lying down;
  you are familiar with all my ways.
4 Before a word is on my tongue
  you, LORD, know it completely.
5 You hem me in behind and before,
  and you lay your hand upon me.
6 Such knowledge is too wonderful for me,
  too lofty for me to attain.

7 Where can I go from your Spirit?
  Where can I flee from your presence?
8 If I go up to the heavens, you are there;
  if I make my bed in the depths, you are
    there.

9 If I rise on the wings of the dawn,
if I settle on the far side of the sea,
10 even there your hand will guide me,
your right hand will hold me fast.
11 If I say, "Surely the darkness will hide me
and the light become night around me,"
12 even the darkness will not be dark to you;
the night will shine like the day,
for darkness is as light to you.

13 For you created my inmost being;
you knit me together in my mother's
womb.
14 I praise you because I am fearfully and
wonderfully made;
your works are wonderful,
I know that full well.
15 My frame was not hidden from you
when I was made in the secret place,
when I was woven together in the depths
of the earth.
16 Your eyes saw my unformed body;
all the days ordained for me were written
in your book
before one of them came to be.
17 How precious to me are your thoughts,
God!
How vast is the sum of them!
18 Were I to count them,
they would outnumber the grains of
sand—
when I awake, I am still with you.

Psalm 139:1–18 NIV

6 | I'm So Scared

I met my husband in my church youth group. He asked me to my senior prom, and we went and had a wonderful time. Then we dated for about six months before he left for college at the Ohio State University, and I left for college in Chicago at the Moody Bible Institute. We dated long-distance for four years, but I visited him every month. We wrote love letters daily and talked multiple times a week on the phone. After I graduated, we got married.

We were married five years before our son was born, followed two years later by the birth of our daughter. During this time, I served in our church and led women's Bible studies. My husband was a deacon for ten years, and we led Bible studies together in our home on Sunday nights. In 2008 I began homeschooling my children, and it was hard to leave home to serve at church, so I began an online ministry called Women Living Well Ministries.

Late one night, I was reading another woman's Christian blog and I thought, *I can do this too.* My husband traveled for work, so when he was gone, I used my spare time to write. I was amazed when women started reading my blog! I wrote devotionals, but I also opened a window into my private life. I wrote openly about my marriage, my parenting struggles, our homeschool days, and the topic of homemaking, all with the gospel in mind, pointing to Jesus.

Before I began blogging, I had begun small groups in my church called Good Morning Girls groups. These were accountability groups for our quiet times, and I shared about these groups on my blog. Women emailed me from all around the world and asked if they could start groups like this too. So I created a newsletter for these women, and Good Morning Girls groups began popping up all across the country. Women were sending me pictures of their groups, and eventually I began getting pictures of groups in other countries and even had women translating my studies into their own language for the women in their church.

This was all God's doing!

I could never have imagined anything like this happening. I was so excited to be able to follow the Great Commission and go into all the world with the gospel through my computer, in my kitchen, from here in Ohio. At that time, Facebook, Twitter, and all the other social media we have now were new or didn't yet exist. So I began a YouTube channel, and somehow a producer of the *Rachael Ray Show* stumbled across one of my very first YouTube videos about marriage. The producer called me and interviewed me over the phone. She wanted to know more about my marriage. I explained to her about Genesis and Ephesians and what God's Word says about marriage and how we tried to live that out in our home.

I guess it was an anomaly to the producer because she asked to send a camera crew to our house and interview us and record me cooking and cleaning, and then they flew me and my husband to New York City, where we appeared on the show for an interview. This was November of 2009.

Appearing on the show brought a lot of attention my way. I ended up with a book deal and speaking opportunities, and my blog grew. My Facebook pages and other social media grew as well. I never dreamt this all would happen. I was not striving or trying to do any of this. God was opening doors, and I was simply walking through them in what I believed was obedience. God had blessed the sharing of his Word, and I was excited to be used by him in this way.

But in 2014, my children were getting near the teenage years, and I felt that they needed some privacy. Blogging can bring a lot of criticism, and they needed to be protected from that. So I began to close the window into my home, and I slowed down on my writings about marriage and family. I began to only focus on writing Bible studies. Little did I know that God was going before me and preparing me for the darkest days of my life.

As I wrote earlier, my husband traveled a lot for work. I believed that I was loved, and I loved him. But in the fall of 2015, I would discover my husband's affair, and by Christmastime we would be separated. I did not want a divorce, but by October of 2016, less than ten months later, I would be divorced. I was in shock. I was still homeschooling my kids and had a ministry online to run, and I did not know what to do.

My life was so public, but a year before God had gone before me and led me to close the window of our day-to-day lives to the public. So I was able to be private while my marriage of nineteen years spiraled downward. Downward until the man I had loved for twenty-four years walked away to a new life path, separate from mine.

The year leading up to that day had been excruciating. There is no way for me to express the level of pain, heartache, and fear that year held. The day after our divorce was final, he bought a second home a couple states away, and a new life of being a single mom began for me.

The Loss of My Marriage Was Devastating

A double blow came the day after my divorce was finalized and I knew it was time to share my truth online. The fear of possible online rejection felt like it might be too much to bear. I thought about all the negative comments I had received over the years over petty things, and I thought that if ever I was going to get some hurtful emails, this was going to be the time. I wasn't sure if I could emotionally handle it, but I knew that I had to hold my ministry with an open hand and trust God.

Deciding how much to share and how much to protect was like walking a tight rope. Since I had one goal, even after my divorce—restoration of my marriage—I knew that less was more. So for various reasons, it was scary to hit publish on that post.

But then it happened. I stood metaphorically naked before all my readers, and they hugged me with their words. Comments, emails, letters, and packages came in, expressing love and prayers, enough to drown out the few painful ones I received.

Facing the Unknown

I had always believed God would take care of me, but never had I been tested in this area. And so waves of fear would sweep over me regularly. Worst-case scenarios would flash through my mind as the joyful, happy life I once knew was gone, and now life simply felt only one way—scary.

If you are going through the worst season of your life, I want you to know that I feel your pain. I know how scary it can be to face the unknown. I know what it's like to worry about the future of your kids, the future of your finances, what everyone is thinking or saying about you behind your back and sometimes to your face, and what it feels like to wonder if you'll ever stop hurting.

Peace, Be Still

In Mark 4, Jesus was sleeping in a boat with his disciples when a storm broke out. Look at what happened.

> And a great windstorm arose, and the waves were breaking into the boat, so that the boat was already filling. But he was in the stern, asleep on the cushion. And they woke him and said to him, "Teacher, do you not care that we are perishing?" And he awoke and rebuked the wind and said to the sea, "Peace! Be still!" And the wind ceased, and there was a great calm. He said to them, "Why are you so afraid? Have you still no faith?" And they were filled with great fear and said to one another, "Who then is this, that even the wind and the sea obey him?"
>
> Mark 4:37–41

In the midst of the storm, the disciples felt like Jesus did not care. But he did. Jesus got up and spoke to the wind and the waves and said, "*Peace! Be still!*" And then he looked at his disciples and essentially asked, *Where is your faith*?

Are you in the midst of a storm today?

Are you tempted to believe the lies of the enemy that say that God does not care?

God cares.

The enemy wants you to be fearful and worried. He wants to keep you in the darkness of these emotions. Do you know what the mix of fear and worry is called?

Anxiety.

Anxiety is rampant in our culture. So many of us struggle with this very strong emotion. When we lack control in life, it is easy to become anxious and fearful of the uncertain outcome.

But when the darkness of fear sweeps over us, that is when we must lean hard on our faith.

Hebrews 11:1 says, "Faith is the assurance of things hoped for."

You see, fear is the dread of an uncertain outcome, but faith has assurance.

Faith is certain.

Faith is confident.

You must let your faith overcome your fears!

And so your faith must grow, but you may ask, How do I grow my faith?

Mine has grown two ways. First, through my private times of prayer and study of God's Word. The deeper I know God and God knows me, the deeper my faith has grown. And second, through wrestling in the darkness and finding that God is right there with me in my darkness. My life experiences have taught me that the more the battle rages, the stronger my faith grows as I experience God holding me up another day. When we are walking with God we can literally withstand anything! Believe that, friend, because that is some serious hope right there.

So what are you fearful about today?

I had to give God all my fears so I could have peace in my soul. Isn't that what we all long for—peace for our soul? God holds it out to us. Peace is available. His Word brings light into the darkness and freedom to those who are gripped with fear and anxiety. His Word has the power to rid you of your anxious thoughts so you can walk in his peace and be free.

When the fear and anxiety were too much, I had to stand in the light of God's Word and chase the darkness of these emotions away. So let me share with you some of the verses I turned to when I was scared. I recommend you mark this page so when hard days hit, you can find these verses quickly. Pray these Scriptures one by one over your life and watch the darkness lift.

Ten Verses for When You Are Scared

1) ***Remember, God is holding you with his hand. He will strengthen you!***

Fear not, for I am with you; be not dismayed, for I am your God; I will strengthen you, I will help you, I will uphold you with my righteous right hand.

Isaiah 41:10

2) ***God is with you wherever you go.***

Have I not commanded you? Be strong and courageous. Do not be frightened, and do not be dismayed, for the Lord your God is with you wherever you go.

Joshua 1:9

3) ***God has given us a spirit of power, love, and self-control, not fear.***

For God gave us a spirit not of fear but of power and love and self-control.

2 Timothy 1:7

4) ***Pray continually to God. His peace will guard you.***

Do not be anxious about anything, but in everything by prayer and supplication with thanksgiving let your requests be made known to God. And the peace of God, which surpasses all understanding, will guard your hearts and your minds in Christ Jesus.

Philippians 4:6–7

5) ***God's peace is above anything that the world can give us.***

Peace I leave with you; my peace I give to you. Not as the world gives do I give to you. Let not your hearts be troubled, neither let them be afraid.

John 14:27

6) ***No matter what you are walking through, allow his presence to comfort you.***

Even though I walk through the valley of the shadow of death, I will fear no evil, for you are with me; your rod and your staff, they comfort me.

Psalm 23:4

7) ***Remember that all things are possible with God!***

But Jesus looked at them and said, "With man this is impossible, but with God all things are possible."

Matthew 19:26

8) ***Spiritual warfare is real. Use your shield of faith! There is power in believing and trusting God.***

In all circumstances take up the shield of faith, with which you can extinguish all the flaming darts of the evil one.

Ephesians 6:16

9) ***When you fully trust in God, you will bear fruit and not be consumed by fear.***

Blessed is the man who trusts in the LORD, whose trust is the LORD. He is like a tree planted by water, that sends out its roots by the stream, and does not fear when heat comes, for its leaves remain green, and is not anxious in the year of drought, for it does not cease to bear fruit.

Jeremiah 17:7–8

10) ***Be self-controlled. Walk in the Spirit so you do not give in to your fears. Spend quality time with God in his Word and in prayer.***

I sought the LORD, and he answered me and delivered me from all my fears.

Psalm 34:4

REFLECTION QUESTIONS

1. What are you fearful or anxious about today?

2. Take a moment to read Psalm 139 on pages 67–68. Record all the times, places, and ways that God is with you.

3. Look back over the list you just wrote above. How does remembering these truths calm your fears and anxious thoughts?

4. In Mark 4:38, the disciples were in a boat in the midst of a huge storm, and Jesus was sleeping. The disciples woke Jesus and asked him, "Do you not care?" Have you ever felt like the disciples? Do you wonder where God is in the midst of life's storms and if he really cares? Why or why not?

5. Which one of the "Ten Verses for When You Are Scared" most resonates with you? Write that verse down on a sticky note or a piece of paper and keep it near you in your car, by your bed, in your bathroom, or in the kitchen. Read it over and over and let God and his Word be a comfort to you this week.

7 | I'm So Angry

I had just left my counseling session, and my heart was filled with sadness. I did not want to go home, so instead I decided to go for a drive. I put all my windows down, turned up the radio loud, and drove. I was headed nowhere. I found some back roads one town over and just drove and drove and drove.

My hair blew all around and I sang loudly to the music and the tears began to flow. My crying turned to sobbing until I could not see the road in front of me and had to pull over.

A mix of sadness and anger washed over me. I banged the steering wheel with my hand. Life was not fair! How could I love and serve God all my life, and God let this happen to me? How could I love my husband faithfully since I was seventeen years old, and he just replace me with another woman? How was I supposed to go on in life without my best friend of twenty-four years? What in the world was I going to do?

How had it come to this? I was never the girl who needed counseling; I was always the girl who helped counsel others. I was the girl who knew the answers, and if I didn't know the answer, I found the answer and gave one. I was the good girl. I obeyed the rules and tried to smile at everyone everywhere I went. I was a try-hard girl. I had tried hard all my life to do everything right and by the book. I didn't want anyone to not like me, but clearly my husband no longer liked me, or perhaps it was just that he liked this other woman more than me.

I was angry. I wanted to quit everything. I was exhausted from the try-hard life. Look where it had gotten me. Alone. Completely alone. There was not one thing I could do to fix this.

I was so confused. One minute he said he missed me and loved me and wanted to be back together, but the next minute he said he needed freedom. Was I supposed to implement boundaries or receive him back in Christian love? There was no handbook with play-by-play instructions for me to follow, and it felt like everyone seemed to know what I should do next except me.

Some people were telling me the way I received him back repeatedly made it appear like I lacked self-worth. I, on the other hand, felt like it was my strength and confidence in the Lord that was helping me to forgive, offer unconditional love, and hold to my vows, *for better or worse*, and we were falling into the category of *worse*.

Being misjudged by others made me angry. Could they not see that I was in the midst of a spiritual battle, and I needed their help to fight? I just wanted support, and the criticism and advice was not helping me. It only confused me more. I loved my husband. Nothing they were going to say was going to stop me from loving him. I know they wanted to shake me and get me to wake up. They could see I was in denial, but I didn't want to be woken up. I wanted them to pray with me, bring me a warm meal, or give me a night off from the kids. None of that was happening.

Darkness had entered our home, and you better believe I was going to fight tooth and nail to keep our marriage together. I felt like there was a target on our backs because we had done so much ministry together, leading Bible studies, doing ministry in our home, serving in our church and online.

I felt that maybe I had caused this spiritual attack because from time to time I had written on marriage on my blog. I was not about to let the enemy win on my watch, and I felt nearly confident we would be reconciled. I knew that this is where my God shines best. He is powerful, and I believed we would, through his power, overcome.

Only that had not happened. The divorce was final, and my ex-husband was a few states away. He was gone, and nothing made sense in my life—absolutely nothing. I felt like someone had stabbed me in the chest. Never had I felt so much pain in my life.

I had a good cry that day. A much-needed sob session. I literally exhausted myself crying so hard. Then I got back on the road, with my worship music playing softly and my mouth completely shut in silence, and I began the long drive home.

Beware, Anger Can Lead to Bitterness

Pain and unanswered questions can lead to bitterness and resentment. Bitterness is ugly. It can fester and cause a lot of trouble if we do not pay attention to the emotion of anger in our life. We must not let it get out of control. This may seem like a strange solution, but the one thing I have learned I need when I am angry is comfort.

> The Lord is close to the brokenhearted and saves those who are crushed in spirit.
>
> Psalm 34:18 NIV

God gave us tear ducts for a reason. Sometimes tears express emotions no words could come close to expressing, and God saw my tears of anger and pain that day. He saw my broken heart, and he was with me. It was freeing to just let the tears flow. It was freeing to say my questions out loud to him. But after I was done crying, I had to go home, and I had to move on.

Moving forward is necessary.

You see, the enemy wants to keep us stuck in our minds in a loop of replaying past hurts, wounds, and pain over and over. If he can keep us stuck, he can get a death grip on us. Staying stuck will cause us to lose our peace, joy, and love and instead be filled with confusion, bitterness, and anger.

It is so easy for my mind to keep looping around and around, trying to make sense of things that don't make sense. I remember talking to my parents, trying to make sense of how my marriage fell apart and asking if they could see it coming. My dad said to me, "Courtney, you are trying to make sense of something that does not make sense, and you can't."

I have repeated those words out loud to my children and friends when I've seen them stuck in that same loop. We can get stuck there for years if we are not careful. I have learned that there are some things on this side of heaven that we will never be able to resolve or tie up neatly in a bow.

Learning to live with things that don't make sense is hard, very hard. But it is possible! Very possible. And Paul tells us to let go of the past and move forward toward God's calling for our lives. We must keep pressing on one day at a time.

> Forgetting what is behind and straining toward what is ahead, I press on toward the goal to win the prize for which God has called me heavenward in Christ Jesus.
>
> Philippians 3:13–14 NIV

Anger Is a Form of Grief

If you are familiar with the five stages of grief, then you know that the final stage of grief is acceptance. We'll talk more about that later in this book. But one of the middle stages of grief is anger. According to the grief cycle, usually before we reach peace and acceptance, we feel the very strong emotion of anger.

You see, anger comes when we experience an injustice. It can be a perceived injustice or a real one. It can come from a loss—like perhaps a friend betrayed you, a boss fired you, your child was overlooked for an award, or your car just broke down after you paid to have it fixed—or it can come from a direct offense, like someone insulting you.

There is sinful anger and there is righteous anger. Righteous anger is being angry at something that angers God. But even when we have righteous anger we are not to sin. Why? Because it gives the enemy a foothold. "'In your anger do not sin': Do not let the sun go down while you are still angry, and do not give the devil a foothold" (Ephesians 4:26–27 NIV).

Beware, when the emotion of anger begins to rear its ugly head; you may be walking right into the enemy's trap. Some people get stuck here and are angry the rest of their lives. The enemy would like to put you in a headlock and just hold you in your state of anger and keep you stuck in the darkness for years. We must break free, and Ephesians 4 says to do it today, before the sun goes down.

What Is the Enemy Using in Your Life to Keep You Stuck?

Are your past wounds holding you hostage and making you bitter?

When our anger is at another person, the key to getting rid of our anger is forgiving that person.

> For if you forgive others their trespasses, your heavenly Father will also forgive you, but if you do not forgive others their trespasses, neither will your Father forgive your trespasses.
>
> Matthew 6:14–15

Oh, how I wish I could delete certain memories from my mind—the command to forgive would be so much easier—but I can't. The reality is, we have all been wounded by people in our lives, and we can either replay those wounds over and over and let bitterness take root and grow in our hearts or we can choose to forgive.

Forgiveness is a choice, an active, intentional choice.

If you are struggling to forgive others who have hurt you, you are not alone. Bitterness can make a heart cold. Do you want to be cold? I don't want to be cold either! I want to grow old gracefully, with a genuine smile of joy that reflects a warm heart of freedom and peace in Christ.

Here Is What Forgiveness Is Not

1) *Forgiveness does not mean we forget.*

While it's humanly impossible to forget the wrongs done to us, we can choose to leave them in the past. Scripture says this is a mature way of thinking.

> But one thing I do: forgetting what lies behind and straining forward to what lies ahead, I press on toward the goal for the prize of the upward call of God in Christ Jesus. Let those of us who are mature think this way.
>
> Philippians 3:13–15

2) *Forgiveness does not equal trust.*

Trust needs to be rebuilt through watching the actions of the offender to see if there has been a true heart change.

> The prudent sees danger and hides himself, but the simple go on and suffer for it.
>
> Proverbs 22:3

3) Forgiveness does not equal reconciliation.

Reconciliation is the goal in a broken relationship, and sometimes when we take the first step to forgive, this leads the other person to repentance and a true heart change. But this is not always the case.

You may offer forgiveness, and the other person may not acknowledge the offense. Perhaps they are happy to receive the forgiveness but in no way are sorry for what they have done, or they apologize but their actions show there has been no true heart change. As a result, the relationship cannot be fully restored.

If we act as though the offense never occurred, trouble will be right around the corner.

> Behold, I am sending you out as sheep in the midst of wolves, so be wise as serpents and innocent as doves.
>
> Matthew 10:16

Jesus told believers to be as innocent as doves—offer forgiveness—but be wise as serpents—be cautious.

4) Forgiveness does not make the offense okay; it makes you okay.

Why forgive?

Forgiveness is good for the soul.

It is the beginning of bringing healing to your heart. When we don't forgive others, our walk with the Lord is hindered. God knows what is best for us, and so he commands us to forgive others just as he has forgiven us.

It's time to leave the hurt and pain in the past with Jesus. We can't drive a car forward by staring in the rearview mirror. Stop looking back. Cry it out if you need to, and then after you are done, look ahead. Move forward. Step out of the darkness and stand in the light. Read, meditate, write out and pray these ten verses over your life, and watch the darkness lift.

Ten Verses for When You Feel Angry

1) *Be silent so you do not sin.*

Be angry, and do not sin; ponder in your own hearts on your beds, and be silent.

Psalm 4:4

2) *Be wise and hold back quietly rather than acting foolishly and venting all of your emotions.*

A fool gives full vent to his spirit, but a wise man quietly holds it back.

Proverbs 29:11

3) *Be slow to anger. Your anger does not produce the righteousness of God.*

Know this, my beloved brothers: let every person be quick to hear, slow to speak, slow to anger; for the anger of man does not produce the righteousness of God.

James 1:19–20

4) *Seek to understand the other person's perspective before reacting defensively.*

Whoever is slow to anger has great understanding, but he who has a hasty temper exalts folly.

Proverbs 14:29

5) *Speak softly and kindly. Do not be harsh.*

A soft answer turns away wrath, but a harsh word stirs up anger.

Proverbs 15:1

6) Do not get involved in controversial conversations that could produce anger.

Have nothing to do with foolish, ignorant controversies; you know that they breed quarrels. And the Lord's servant must not be quarrelsome but kind to everyone, able to teach, patiently enduring evil.

2 Timothy 2:23–24

7) God will repay; it is not up to you to punish someone for wrongdoing.

Beloved, never avenge yourselves, but leave it to the wrath of God, for it is written, "Vengeance is mine, I will repay, says the Lord."

Romans 12:19

8) Look for opportunities to do good in the midst of a problem.

Do not be overcome by evil, but overcome evil with good.

Romans 12:21

9) Extend forgiveness to those who have sinned against you.

Let all bitterness and wrath and anger and clamor and slander be put away from you, along with all malice. Be kind to one another, tenderhearted, forgiving one another, as God in Christ forgave you.

Ephesians 4:31–32

10) Live out the fruit of the Spirit in your life so you do not give in to your anger.

But the fruit of the Spirit is love, joy, peace, patience, kindness, goodness, faithfulness, gentleness, self-control; against such things there is no law.

Galatians 5:22–23

REFLECTION QUESTIONS

1. When was the last time you felt very angry? What did you say or do? Was this righteous anger or unrighteous anger?

2. Are you still angry right now because of a wound from the past? Who or what is the enemy using in your life to keep you stuck in bitterness?

3. Look at Matthew 6:14–15. Why should we forgive others who have wronged us?

4. Is there someone in your life you need to forgive? In what ways do you find this statement to be true: "Forgiveness is a choice, an active, intentional choice"?

5. Which one of the "Ten Verses for When You Feel Angry" most resonates with you? Write the verse below and on a slip of paper. Consider committing this verse to memory this week.

8 I'm So Embarrassed

I was at a conference with nearly a thousand women in attendance. I had just finished speaking in my small session and went into the large room next door, where a famous author was on the stage speaking. The speaker looked my direction and said, "Let me introduce you to someone who is amazing at marketing—my good friend Courtney. Courtney, please stand up."

My heart started beating fast. She was looking at me, and in my mind I was thinking, *Wow, she just called me a good friend. We just met yesterday.*

So I stood up like a peacock, all smiles! Heads cranked around and looked at me. Then it happened . . .

I realized another girl was standing too! The speaker went on to explain that *Courtney* gave her a great idea for the marketing of her new book. I had given her *no* ideas for the marketing of her book. I dropped down like a bullet to my seat, and as I dropped down, I tipped my cup that was full of water, and it went everywhere. Now everyone who cranked their necks around could see I was a mess! I slipped out the back door and ran to the bathroom to get paper towels, and in the bathroom, I looked at myself in the mirror and said, "Girl—why in the world did you stand? You know you aren't good friends with that famous author! And who is this other Courtney girl?"

Hoping not too many people noticed, I went on to other sessions in the conference, trying to recover. Later I got on Twitter, and the other Courtney had tweeted, "Giggling over the Courtney confusion today. Will the real Courtney please stand up? Heehee!" Oh, my goodness, people did notice! She saw me and she tweeted about it.

Later I saw the speaker, and I wondered, did she see me stand like a peacock? Oh yes, yes, she did! I mean how could you miss it? She said, "Courtney, I am so sorry! I just didn't know how to recover for you!"

I Was So Embarrassed

Later I got to spend some time at a breakfast table with the speaker, getting to know her a little better, and when we parted ways on the last day, she looked at me and said, "Now I can truly say *my good friend Courtney*."

We all experience embarrassing moments like these. They are the kind of stories that in the moment seem horrifying but later we laugh when we retell the story.

This type of embarrassing moment was nothing compared to the embarrassment I felt when my husband left me for another woman. I felt like a failure. I felt ugly. I felt stupid. I felt gullible. I felt like a fraud. I felt like never showing my face again in church.

And So, I Hid

For five years leading up to my husband leaving me, he and I worked together in the nursery every other Sunday morning during the first hour of church. Then we went to the second service to worship in the sanctuary. Conveniently, we had just stepped down from volunteering before the holidays, and so after he left me, I had no desire to join an adult Sunday school class during that first hour. Instead, I dropped my kids off for youth group, and then I went to a local coffee shop to get a cup of coffee and read my Bible. Then I would return to church, slip into the back row in the darkness of our gymnasium to attend an overflow service, and slip out quickly.

I wanted to be alone.

I did not have the capacity to connect with others. During this season I feared that the very simple question of "How are you doing this morning?" would lead to me either crying or lying and saying I was okay when I was not okay.

I hid.

I wanted to be alone, and yet I did not want to be alone. I chose to isolate myself for self-preservation reasons. I felt safer.

Shame

Shame on me for not being a good enough wife to be able to keep my husband. Shame on me for not realizing he was being unfaithful. How in the world did I miss the red flags? Shame on me for taking him back over and over and letting him repeat his unfaithfulness to me. Shame on me for getting a divorce. You know God hates divorce. Shame on me for isolating myself and not going to Sunday school or connecting with the church body when I knew that I should be connecting and serving.

Shame will take you down the darkest road of your life if you let it. It will suffocate you if you do not break free. How do I know? Because I felt it with every fiber of my being. For almost two years straight, I sat at that coffee shop alone, hiding in my shame.

Over a year and a half in, a compassionate friend invited me to her Sunday school class at my church. She worked on me for a while to finally get me there. She assured me that she would sit with me so I would not be alone. It was a parenting class, and she knew I needed that as a new single mom. I was scared. Imagine! I, who had gone to church since I was three weeks old, who had gone to Bible college, and who loved church—and literally never missed a Sunday all my life unless I was throwing up over a toilet—was scared to death to show my face in my church.

Spiritual Warfare Is Real

Satan did not want me back in church. It was strange how my church went from feeling like home and family to feeling like it was a country club and I did not fit in. Everyone seemed so put together, just like I used to be. I felt exposed, as I knew people knew the mess my life had become, and I was embarrassed.

I sat in that Sunday school class, and the teachers were wonderful godly men and the teaching was spot-on, so this is not on them, but I did not fit. All their teaching was geared at parenting in a two-parent home. They asked if anyone had any questions. I raised my hand. They had been talking about limiting the use of cell phones with our children, and I shared my predicament of how I was able to do this in my home but when my children were at their father's house, I wasn't sure how to handle that.

Everyone was looking at me.

That hot feeling came over me like the feeling I'd had back at that conference when everyone had turned around, staring at me. *Why in the world did I ask that question?* I had just outed myself from hiding and revealed myself as the only single mom in the room. I had just done the very thing I was trying to avoid. I was so embarrassed; I left the class that day and did not return.

Shame Causes Us to Hide

Shame began in the garden of Eden. After Adam and Eve sinned, they hid from God. They went from feeling safe and secure to feeling exposed, and so they hid.

Shame can come when we fear being exposed or have already been exposed. Shame can cause us not to trust those around us and to withdraw from others. As a result, we may feel even more self-conscious and fearful as we hide from others.

I have experienced all of the above, and if you have too, you are not alone. We must let God's light shine into this darkness. Remember, we are more than conquerors.

The Woman at the Well

The name of my online ministry is Women Living Well Ministries. I named it after the woman at the well's experience with Jesus, when he told her that after she drank from the well, she would be thirsty again. Then he offered her living water from which she would never thirst again.

I believe women will live well when they drink from the living well, the living waters of God. And so I started a ministry online in 2008 to encourage women to drink from the living well. In no way could I have foreseen when I started the ministry that I would one day be a single mom and experience the shame I have experienced.

Suddenly this passage of Scripture took on a whole new meaning. Look at the background story to this unnamed woman at the well.

> Jesus answered, "Everyone who drinks this water will be thirsty again, but whoever drinks the water I give them will never thirst. Indeed, the water I give them will become in them a spring of water welling up to eternal life."
>
> The woman said to him, "Sir, give me this water so that I won't get thirsty and have to keep coming here to draw water."
>
> He told her, "Go, call your husband and come back."
>
> "I have no husband," she replied.
>
> Jesus said to her, "You are right when you say you have no husband. The fact is, you have had five husbands, and the man you now have is not your husband. What you have just said is quite true."
>
> John 4:13–18 NIV

Earlier in this passage, we are told that this woman went completely alone to the well in the heat of the day. Usually in their culture, women went in the morning in the cool of the day. Perhaps what men had done to her or women had said about her or the choices she had regrettably made led her to hide.

Scripture says she had suffered five broken marriages, and it was at her rock bottom, when she was isolated and all alone, that Jesus met her and completely changed her life. That's our God! He loves the brokenhearted.

He Is With Us

Jesus knew exactly why the woman was hiding, and so he immediately brought her darkness to light. He told her to go get her husband. She answered that she did not have a husband, and then Jesus said she was right—she'd had five husbands, and the man she was now with was not her husband.

This was a divine appointment. Jesus called her out. He called her out of darkness and into the light. She had spent her life seeking a man who would never leave her, forsake her, reject her, or betray her and had come up empty, but now she met Jesus. Her eyes were opened, and she realized she was speaking to the Messiah. She dropped her jar and ran back into town to tell others about him.

The unnamed woman at the well stopped hiding and became an evangelist! The passage says, "Many of the Samaritans from that town believed in him because of the woman's testimony" (John 4:39 NIV). Many believed because of the woman's testimony. Friend, Jesus wants to use you and your story in the same way. He wants to set you free!

Perhaps you have hurt others in your past and caused a relationship to be severed, or maybe you have been hurt, rejected, or abandoned by someone who was supposed to love you. Maybe a mother or father, sister or brother, spouse or close friend has done unthinkable things to you, and that relationship is now broken.

You see, many of us hide in different ways. Some hide in good books, bingeing on movies, or continual scrolling online. Others of us hide in our work, our kids, our homes, our food, or in our busy schedules. But there is only one hiding place where we can become completely healed and saved from our sin and shame—Jesus.

Jesus is our safe refuge.

He is our living well!

> Looking to Jesus, *the founder and perfecter of our faith*, who for the joy that was set before him endured the cross, despising the shame, *and is seated at the right hand of the throne of God*. Consider him who endured from sinners such hostility *against himself*, so that you may not grow weary or fainthearted.
>
> Hebrews 12:2–3, emphasis added

Look to Jesus. He wants to restore you and remove all of your shame. He died so you could live free! Let him be your refuge and strength today.

God Is the Creator of Love

He *is* love, and his love for you has no end. Over and over, we are told in Scripture and shown in Scripture that God loves us.

Our doubts do not change God's love for us.

Our fears do not change God's love for us.

Our shame does not change God's love for us.

His love is steadfast and constant. When you are God's child—no matter what you do, good or bad—he still loves you.

It's time for the darkness to flee and for you to stand in the light of God's Word. On days when you feel like the shame and embarrassment of your circumstances are too much and you need to be reminded of God's deep love for you, read, meditate, write out, and pray these verses over your life. Once again, I recommend you mark this page so when hard days hit you can find it again quickly. Pray these verses one by one over your life and watch the darkness lift.

Ten Verses about God's Love For You

1) ***God is love!***

Beloved, let us love one another, for love is from God, and whoever loves has been born of God and knows God. Anyone who does not love does not know God, because God is love.

1 John 4:7–8

2) ***No one has a greater love for you than Jesus!***

Greater love has no one than this, that someone lay down his life for his friends.

John 15:13

3) ***Nothing can ever separate you from God's love.***

In all these things we are more than conquerors through him who loved us. For I am sure that neither death nor life, nor angels nor rulers, nor things present nor things to come, nor powers, nor height nor depth, nor anything else in all creation, will be able to separate us from the love of God in Christ Jesus our Lord.

Romans 8:37–39

4) ***God is with you. Let him quiet your restless heart with his love.***

The Lord your God is in your midst, a mighty one who will save; he will rejoice over you with gladness; he will quiet you by his love; he will exult over you with loud singing.

Zephaniah 3:17

5) ***God loves you so much he gave his only Son, so you could have eternal life.***

For God so loved the world, that he gave his only Son, that whoever believes in him should not perish but have eternal life.

John 3:16

6) ***God calls you his child.***

See what kind of love the Father has given to us, that we should be called children of God; and so we are.

1 John 3:1

7) ***God is slow to anger and abounding in steadfast love toward you.***

But you, O Lord, are a God merciful and gracious, slow to anger and abounding in steadfast love and faithfulness.

Psalm 86:15

8) ***He is your loving father. His discipline shows his love for you.***

For the Lord disciplines the one he loves, and chastises every son whom he receives.

Hebrews 12:6

9) ***God demonstrated his love for you through the death of Christ.***

But God shows his love for us in that while we were still sinners, Christ died for us.

Romans 5:8

10) ***God's love for you endures forever. It never ends!***

Give thanks to the God of heaven, for his steadfast love endures forever.

Psalm 136:26

REFLECTION QUESTIONS

1. Think back over your life. Are there any regrets or wounds that the enemy has used to make you feel shame? What happened? In what ways did the enemy lie to you during that time?

2. Alone time is not bad. It is needed to refresh and restore our souls. But if we are isolating ourselves because we are hiding from shame, the enemy can use that isolation to keep us trapped in darkness. Some of us hide in our work, our kids, our homes, our food, our busy schedules, reading books, bingeing on movies, or continually scrolling online. In what unhealthy ways do you tend to hide?

3. Look at the story of the woman at the well. Note that the woman at the well is unnamed. She was a social outcast. How was her life transformed by her encounter with Jesus?

4. How has your life been transformed by your encounter with Jesus?

5. Turn to Hebrews 12:2–3 and read it slowly and out loud if you can. How could really believing the words of these verses transform your life?

9 | I'm So Worried

I used to have this pink shirt with black letters that read *Warrior not Worrier*. The last time I cleaned out my closet I got rid of it. I could not confidently walk around the house in this shirt. My kids would have fallen on the floor laughing at me. For the first twelve years of their lives, I was homeschooling them, so I did not worry too much about them. But after their father left and they started school, I was worried.

I was constantly trying to keep tabs on where they were going and who they were with. I wanted to know what music they were listening to and what books they were reading, and I did not want them on social media. I purchased an app to protect them on the internet, and I had them plug their phones in at night in the kitchen so I could peek at their text messages. Then I worried that this parenting style might be messing my kids up!

I worried that they did not have a father in the home. I wondered if going from homeschooling to brick-and-mortar school was the right decision. I worried when they visited youth groups of their friends and came back liking other churches more than ours. I worried about them wanting to leave our church. I worried when my son's friends were all allowed to play video games and he was not. I wanted him to fit in. It was during the Covid outbreak, when we were all quarantined in our homes and they were bored out of their minds, that I began to bend my rules and allow them to use social media and video games a lot more freely. And then I worried that this parenting style might be messing them up too!

Then they began to drive, and as their freedoms grew so did my worries. I worried about them out on the roads late at night. I worried about who they were dating. I worried about their life goals and their spiritual lives. And then it happened. My oldest child graduated and went off to college two states away, and his sister followed him to the same college one year later. Talk about giving a mom something to worry about! My babies were launched, and all I could do was pray and hope for the best.

Being a mom is hard.

What Is Worry?

The word *worry* can be both a verb and a noun. In the verb form, the Merriam-Webster dictionary definition includes these descriptions—"to afflict with mental distress or agitation, to harass by tearing, biting or snapping . . . to touch or disturb something repeatedly, torment, choke, strangle"—and in the noun form its definition includes "mental distress and anxiety."[1]

Are you a worrier?

Essentially, worry is the act of tormenting yourself with disturbing thoughts. Are you tormenting yourself with disturbing thoughts? Are you being choked by your anxiety? Do you think about, talk about, and dwell long on things that are troubling you?

Or are you a warrior?

The opposite of being a worrier is a warrior. A warrior is a brave fighter. A warrior has courage and is not passive. A warrior is engaged in battle and sacrifices for the good of others.

Which do you want to be? It seems obvious, and yet, it feels like worry is only natural, and as soon as we find peace in one area, a new thing pops up to worry about. The enemy never gives up on attacking us with thoughts that disturb us. We must fight back!

The Example of Ruth

There are only two books in the Bible named after women: Ruth and Esther. Both had a brave warrior spirit despite having a lot to worry about.

Let's take a closer look at the life of Ruth.

In chapter 1 of the book of Ruth, Ruth's husband died, her father-in-law died, she had no children, and she moved to a new land with her mother-in-law, Naomi. I cannot imagine the amount of grief and fear she must have been experiencing at this time.

Then in chapter 2, Ruth and Naomi were in a bad position. They were destitute and needed food to stay alive, and so Ruth's warrior spirit kicked in. Ruth took the initiative to go to a field nearby and worked hard all day long, collecting grain in the hot sun. Then she worked into the late evening, pounding out the grain she had collected. When she was done, she carried her very heavy load of grain all the way home. While God was providing for Ruth, Ruth was working hard to provide for Naomi.

Now remember, Ruth was in a new land with her mother-in-law, so she had no idea whose field she had been working in. In God's sovereignty, it turned out that the field belonged to a close relative named Boaz, who could fulfill the Hebrew law of kinsman-redeemer—essentially, he could rescue her from poverty and protect her through marriage.

God was orchestrating a beautiful love story in the life of Ruth.

So in chapter 3, Ruth took a very risky step forward. Her only hope out of her desperate situation was for this godly man named Boaz to take notice of her and marry her. Naomi gave her instructions according to what was customary in those times. She told Ruth to hide and watch Boaz as he ate and drank alongside his servants. Then once he lay down to sleep, she was to go and lie at his feet.

Ruth's warrior spirit kicked in as she did exactly as Naomi instructed. I am sure her heart was beating fast as she admired him from afar, watching and waiting—waiting on Boaz not only to lie down but to fall asleep. The minutes and hours must have felt like days passing.

Ruth had reason to worry!

Boaz could have rejected her and shamed her. Her reputation as a godly woman could have been damaged. Her assignment from Naomi required a warrior spirit.

And I wonder, What assignment has God given you that requires a warrior spirit?

Ruth understood that Naomi knew God and his Word and that asking Boaz to redeem her was the right thing to do. So she did it!

She went to the threshing floor where Boaz was sleeping, she uncovered his feet, and she lay down. Then Boaz awakened in the night, and he was startled to find her there. Ruth then asked him to redeem her, and chapter 3 ends with Ruth returning home to Naomi as she awaits an answer from Boaz.

Can you imagine? She just proposed to this man, and he did not give her an immediate answer. Instead, he had her hold out her apron, and he filled it with barley and then sent her home before anyone else saw her.

As Ruth patiently waited for his answer, she continued to lean into her warrior spirit. She had plenty to worry about, but she did not give way to fear; instead she trusted God.

In the fourth and final chapter of the book, God worked mightily. Ruth and Boaz not only got married, but they also had a baby together.

Look what God did for Ruth! Ruth's life had been riddled with stress. The death of her husband, a move to a new land, poverty, and hard labor were just some of what she faced, but Ruth's trust in God was revealed through her ability to put one foot in front of the other and do the next hard thing.

What Is the Next Hard Thing You Need to Do?

It's easy to let disturbing thoughts enter our minds. All day long there are many things we could torment ourselves with, but God wants us to trust him. You see, trusting God and worry are like oil and vinegar. They do not mix.

Remember, in Matthew 6:34 (NIV) Jesus commands us, "Do not worry about tomorrow, for tomorrow will worry about itself. Each day has enough trouble of its own."

Are you worrying about tomorrow?

Jesus says not to do this. He wants us to live in the present. The temptation to worry is never going to go away. There are always going to be things in your life that you *could* worry about. Jesus knows this about us, and so he wants us to focus on today and take it just one day at a time.

Worry Is a Choice

Ruth was at peace as she fiercely trusted in God, and God was faithful. He used the darkest days of her life to set the stage for her greatest blessings. Ruth could not see any of this coming during her trials. She made the choice to simply trust in the Lord, and he blessed her in the end.

Friend, God is always at work in our lives in multiple ways that we cannot see. Trust that he is at work in your life and working all things together for good. Perhaps some of your darkest days will lead to your greatest blessings as well. God is faithful. Do not surrender to your worry or get stuck in it. Instead, make the choice today to fight hard to be free.

When the enemy is coming at you with disturbing thoughts, prayer and meditation are the keys to breaking free. These verses below have been a light in the darkness when I have wrestled with worry. Again, I recommend you mark this page so when hard days come, you can find these verses quickly. They will help you rise up and overcome the enemy.

Ten Verses for Battling Worry

1) *Remember to pray. Prayer leads to peace.*

Do not be anxious about anything, but in everything by prayer and supplication with thanksgiving let your requests be made known to God. And the peace of God, which surpasses all understanding, will guard your hearts and your minds in Christ Jesus.

Philippians 4:6–7

2) *God is with us. No matter what we face, we have a future hope that does not disappoint.*

For I know the plans I have for you, declares the Lord, plans for welfare and not for evil, to give you a future and a hope.

Jeremiah 29:11

3) *Throw your burdens on God.*

Cast your burden on the Lord, and he will sustain you; he will never permit the righteous to be moved.

Psalm 55:22

4) *Trust that God is leading you on the path that is best for you.*

Trust in the LORD with all your heart, and do not lean on your own understanding. In all your ways acknowledge him, and he will make straight your paths.

Proverbs 3:5–6

5) *When you feel fear welling up inside of you, stop—put your trust in God.*

When I am afraid, I put my trust in you.

Psalm 56:3

6) *Remember, you are not alone. God is with you.*

Fear not, for I am with you; be not dismayed, for I am your God; I will strengthen you, I will help you, I will uphold you with my righteous right hand.

Isaiah 41:10

7) *Have faith. God will take care of you.*

Therefore I tell you, do not be anxious about your life, what you will eat or what you will drink, nor about your body, what you will put on. Is not life more than food, and the body more than clothing? Look at the birds of the air: they neither sow nor reap nor gather into barns, and yet your heavenly Father feeds them. Are you not of more value than they? And which of you by being anxious can add a single hour to his span of life? And why are you anxious about clothing? Consider the lilies of the field, how they grow: they neither toil nor spin, yet I tell you, even Solomon in all his glory was not arrayed like one of these. But if God so clothes the grass of the field, which today is alive and tomorrow is thrown into the oven, will he not much more clothe you, O you of little faith?

Matthew 6:25–30

8) Each day has enough trouble, so stay focused on today and do not worry about tomorrow.

Do not be anxious about tomorrow, for tomorrow will be anxious for itself. Sufficient for the day is its own trouble.

Matthew 6:34

9) Worry will weigh you down. Words have power. Speak words of truth and encouragement to others and yourself.

Anxiety in a man's heart weighs him down, but a good word makes him glad.

Proverbs 12:25

10) Call on the Lord. He is on your side!

Out of my distress I called on the LORD; the LORD answered me and set me free. The LORD is on my side; I will not fear. What can man do to me?

Psalm 118:5–6

REFLECTION QUESTIONS

1. Look at the descriptions of worry again on page 100. List the ways that worry affects you.
2. Take inventory of your life. What are you worried about right now?
3. Read Matthew 6:34. What does Jesus say about worry, and how can you apply this to the things you are currently worried about?
4. Ruth had an assignment that required a warrior spirit. What assignment has God given you that requires

a warrior spirit, and how can you live that out more today?

5. Worry begins in the mind and is often battled out in prayer. Look over the "Ten Verses for Battling Worry." Choose the verse that most speaks to you and write it out in prayer form, then pray it over your life.

10 I'm So Sad

I know some people believe that the appropriate time to start Christmas music is December 1st. I'm not one of them. You know the type of girl who starts her Christmas music on November 1st and then leaves her Christmas tree up into the New Year? That's me! I'm *that* girl.

I love Christmas. I love the music, the decorations, the get-togethers, the gift giving, the cookies, the cards in the mailbox, the outdoor lights, the choir concerts, and celebrating the birth of Jesus. I love it all! Every single bit of it.

But after my husband left, Christmas changed.

He left on December 22nd. So after he left, every year leading up to that date I began to experience a tidal wave of sadness washing over me. I would be in the grocery store, and the Christmas music playing over the loudspeaker would hit me hard. One time I left my cart of groceries in the store and ran out to my car because I was starting to cry. I was so very sad, and it was like all my Christmas memories had been painted with a dark, sad paintbrush.

As time went on, I found many of my other memories started feeling that way too. I had been into scrapbooking when my kids were little. My husband told me I could spend freely on my scrapbooks because he wanted our memories archived well. He even supported me going on scrapbooking retreats overnight. I would take all my photos from vacations, birthdays, and holidays and spend forty-eight hours putting them beautifully onto the pages of our albums. When I arrived home from scrapbooking retreats, we'd all sit down as a family and enjoy looking at what I had accomplished.

But after he left, suddenly all my albums—full of happy memories—made me sad. It hurt to look at the albums. Questions would run through my mind as I looked at my husband smiling in the pictures. *Was he truly happy in those pictures? Was his smile real? Did he really ever love me? How did this happen?*

Emotional Pain

Sadness is an emotion we all experience when we face disappointment and loss. Sadness is a pain on the inside that can make us feel very lonely even when surrounded by friends and family, especially if they are unaware of how sad we are feeling. Sadness slows us down, changes our countenance, and makes it hard to take even one small step forward.

I've heard it said that sadness and depression come from focusing on the past, and worry and anxiety come from focusing on the future. When we are overwhelmed with sadness, it does us well to have a good crying session. We need to get our sadness out, and God gave us tear ducts for a reason. Tears express emotions that words could never express.

But what do you do when sadness is overwhelming you? Perhaps an exciting pregnancy turned into a miscarriage, or a routine checkup turned into a discovery of cancer. Or maybe a typical car ride turned into a wreck where a loved one was lost, or a normal phone call turned into the last phone call you'd ever receive from a loved one. I've watched friends walk through every single one of these things. Life can be so very sad.

We wonder, Is God really in control of everything?

When storms hit and trials come into our lives, raw emotions bubble up under the surface and begin to overflow. We begin to ask God questions, and we wonder, Does God care? Does God love me? Is he in control?

Yes, a thousand times yes!

Every page of Scripture points to a loving, sovereign God. From the creation account in Genesis to the return of Christ in Revelation, our God is in complete control.

The Example of Job

There's a book in the Old Testament named after a man named Job. Job was an upright, blameless man. God allowed trouble from the hands of the enemy to enter his life, and suddenly Job's world began to unravel and fall apart. His children died, his oxen died, his sheep died, his donkeys died, and he became very sick.

In chapter 1, after the loss of his children and livestock, Job did not shake his fist at God. Instead, he worshiped God. He accepted the sovereignty of God in his life when he said, "The Lord gave, and the Lord has taken away; blessed be the name of the Lord" (Job 1:21).

In chapter 2, after Job became sick, his wife told him to curse God and die. Job refused and instead affirmed the sovereignty of God once again when he responded to his wife, "'Shall we receive good from God, and shall we not receive evil?' In all this Job did not sin with his lips" (Job 2:10).

But in chapter 3, Job began to struggle with the darkness.

He did not curse God, but he cursed the day he was born and fell into sadness and despair. Job did not face sadness and despair because of something he had done wrong. It was the opposite. Chapter 1 tells us he faced all his losses *because* of his faithfulness to God.

Why?

For thirty-five chapters, we see Job repeatedly ask God *why*. Sometimes we can feel the same way. We beg God to let us in on the big picture of *why*. It seems that coping would be much easier if we could just get some answers. And when answers don't come, we can fall into despair.

Then Job's friend Bildad told Job to get right with God and plead for mercy. This was not helpful! He needed compassion, not judgment, from his close friend. And so Job wavered between hope, doubt, and despair. He felt innocent but wondered if God saw him differently.

Have you been there?

Have you wondered why God has allowed you to suffer various trials of different kinds?

Fear
Doubt
Worry
Anxiety
Sadness
Sleepless nights
Unanswered prayers

The enemy has used all of the above to put a death grip on me and threaten to destroy my hope and joy. He hates me, and he hates you. He wants us trapped in these dark emotions: "Your enemy the devil prowls around like a roaring lion looking for someone to devour" (1 Peter 5:8 NIV).

But this I know.

I know that God is good.

I know I can trust in God's goodness even when what I am facing is *not* good.

I know there are pastors on television who say God only wants to see us happy, healthy, and wealthy. This is a lie. We cannot look a cancer patient in the eye or a paralyzed woman bound in a wheelchair for life and say this to them. The Bible is clear that in this world there will be suffering (John 16:33), but heaven awaits us, and one day there will be no more sadness or pain (Revelation 21:4). That is our hope!

Is there an area in your life where you are questioning God and wondering why?

Perhaps your trial is *because* of your faithfulness.

Your trial may exist so that as you worship through tears, Satan is put to shame and God is glorified and honored by your unwavering faithfulness.

God Speaks in the Darkness

Some of my favorite chapters in the Bible are found at the end of the book of Job when God finally began to answer Job. God put his power on display and put an end to Job's questioning.

Here's a taste of some of what God said in response to Job:

> Where were you when I laid the foundation of the earth?
>   Tell me, if you have understanding.
> Who determined its measurements—surely you know!
>   Or who stretched the line upon it?
> On what were its bases sunk,
>   or who laid its cornerstone,
> when the morning stars sang together
>   and all the sons of God shouted for joy?
>
> Job 38:4–7

Have you entered the storehouses of the snow,
    or have you seen the storehouses of the hail,
which I have reserved for the time of trouble,
    for the day of battle and war?
What is the way to the place where the light is
    distributed,
    or where the east wind is scattered upon the earth?

Job 38:22–24

Can you hunt the prey for the lion,
    or satisfy the appetite of the young lions,
when they crouch in their dens
    or lie in wait in their thicket?
Who provides for the raven its prey,
    when its young ones cry to God for help,
    and wander about for lack of food?

Job 38:39–41

Do you give the horse his might?
    Do you clothe his neck with a mane?
Do you make him leap like the locust?
    His majestic snorting is terrifying.
He paws in the valley and exults in his strength;
    he goes out to meet the weapons.
He laughs at fear and is not dismayed;
    he does not turn back from the sword.
Upon him rattle the quiver,
    the flashing spear, and the javelin.
With fierceness and rage he swallows the ground;
    he cannot stand still at the sound of the trumpet.
When the trumpet sounds, he says "Aha!"
    He smells the battle from afar,
    the thunder of the captains, and the shouting.

Job 39:19–25

Do you find comfort in God's response to Job? I do.

God did not just create the heavens and the earth, but he is continually sustaining the heavens and the earth. That's our God! He is with us! The book of Job not only reveals God's sovereignty but also reveals his power, might, grandeur, and wisdom.

There is no one like our God!

And so you may ask one of the most difficult theological questions anyone can ask: Why does God allow sadness and suffering?

Oh, friend, I do not want to pretend to fully understand the answer to this question, nor do I want to give trite answers. But when God spoke, he did not answer Job's questions of *why*. Instead, he reminded Job of how great, powerful, mighty, and good he is. He put all his sovereignty on display, and in chapter 40, Job put his hand over his mouth and went silent.

When we truly see how powerful our God is, our questions are silenced and we can simply rest in him. God existed before the creation of the world. He brought the universe into existence. He is in control. It is through good and evil that we see his full character on display. We see his wrath, his justice, his deep love, mercy, and grace. We would not understand the depths of the kindness and forgiveness of God if we were not being saved from our sins.

Evil came from Satan and the fall in the garden of Eden. We have all sinned. God has allowed evil so we can understand the magnitude of his love and that he might be glorified forever when, in the end, he triumphs over evil.

It is not answers to the questions of *why* that we need. It is God that we need. God *is* the answer! Whatever you are facing today, you can rest in God's love and care for you.

Your trials are meant to point you to God.

Your suffering is meant to point you to God.

Your losses are meant to point you to God.

Your sadness is meant to point you to God.

Why? Because God knows *he* is your greatest need, and when you have *him*, you can have peace and joy in the midst of your pain and sorrow.

Our trials remind us that this world is not our home. We are just passing through. Our life is but a vapor. It is short, and eternity is forever.

In the End, God Triumphs over Evil!

This world is broken. Satan seeks to strip you of your joy and your confidence in God. Fight back, friend! Don't let the enemy lie to you.

If you are tired of crying, take comfort in this: Revelation 21:4 tells us that in heaven there will be no more tears. We have a wonderful hope in Jesus. So when you are tempted to look back in sadness or tempted to look ahead with anxiety, instead look all the way to eternity with hope, and stand today on the sure promises of God. He loves you, and he will never leave you nor forsake you (Deuteronomy 31:6).

Read these verses below often. Step out of the darkness, and let the Lord strengthen you with the light of his Word.

Ten Verses for When You Feel Sad

1) *God sees your tears and sleepless nights. He is for you.*

> You have kept count of my tossings; put my tears in your bottle. Are they not in your book? Then my enemies will turn back in the day when I call. This I know, that God is for me.
>
> Psalm 56:8–9

2) *If you have a friend who is sad, cry with her.*

> Rejoice with those who rejoice, weep with those who weep.
>
> Romans 12:15

3) ***It's okay to cry. Even Jesus cried after the death of his friend.***

Jesus wept.

John 11:35

4) ***God comforts us in our troubles so that we can be a comfort to others when they face troubles.***

Praise be to the God and Father of our Lord Jesus Christ, the Father of compassion and the God of all comfort, who comforts us in all our troubles, so that we can comfort those in any trouble with the comfort we ourselves receive from God.

2 Corinthians 1:3–4 NIV

5) ***Hold on to hope. There will be no more crying or pain in heaven.***

He will wipe every tear from their eyes. There will be no more death or mourning or crying or pain, for the old order of things has passed away.

Revelation 21:4 NIV

6) ***Our sadness is temporary and only for a season. Hang on because joy is coming.***

Weeping may tarry for the night, but joy comes with the morning.

Psalm 30:5

7) ***Cry out to God. Tell him your feelings—list your troubles to him!***

O Lord, all my longing is before you; my sighing is not hidden from you.

Psalm 38:9

8) ***Know that God hears you and is your refuge and strength.***

Cast all your anxiety on him because he cares for you.

1 Peter 5:7 NIV

9) Lift your eyes to him! Seek God for help. Don't look to this world for it.

I lift up my eyes to the hills. From where does my help come? My help comes from the Lord, who made heaven and earth.

Psalm 121:1–2

10) Walk in the Spirit so that you do not allow sadness to control you. Spend quality time with God in his Word and in prayer.

And the Lord will guide you continually and satisfy your desire in scorched places and make your bones strong; and you shall be like a watered garden, like a spring of water, whose waters do not fail.

Isaiah 58:11

REFLECTION QUESTIONS

1. When was the last time you cried or felt very overwhelmed with sadness?

2. Did your sadness cause you to doubt that God cares for you or cause you to question why God would allow you to suffer in this way? Why or why not?

3. Look at God's response to Job's suffering in Job chapters 38 and 39. What do you learn about God from these chapters in Scripture?

4. In what ways does God's response to Job bring you comfort?

5. Look at the "Ten Verses for When You Feel Sad." Second Corinthians 1:3–4 is on the list. How does God say

he wants to use our sadness? Is there someone in your life today who you can be a comfort to? Name them, say a prayer for them now, and write down one way you can encourage them this week.

PART 3

STANDING IN THE LIGHT

[1] The LORD is my light and my salvation—
  whom shall I fear?
The LORD is the stronghold of my life—
  of whom shall I be afraid?

[2] When the wicked advance against me
  to devour me,
it is my enemies and my foes
  who will stumble and fall.
[3] Though an army besiege me,
  my heart will not fear;
though war break out against me,
  even then I will be confident.

[4] One thing I ask from the LORD,
  this only do I seek:
that I may dwell in the house of the LORD
  all the days of my life,
to gaze on the beauty of the LORD
  and to seek him in his temple.
[5] For in the day of trouble
  he will keep me safe in his dwelling;

he will hide me in the shelter of his sacred tent
and set me high upon a rock.

[6] Then my head will be exalted
above the enemies who surround me;
at his sacred tent I will sacrifice with shouts of joy;
I will sing and make music to the LORD.

[7] Hear my voice when I call, LORD;
be merciful to me and answer me.
[8] My heart says of you, "Seek his face!"
Your face, LORD, I will seek.
[9] Do not hide your face from me,
do not turn your servant away in anger;
you have been my helper.
Do not reject me or forsake me,
God my Savior.
[10] Though my father and mother forsake me,
the LORD will receive me.
[11] Teach me your way, LORD;
lead me in a straight path
because of my oppressors.
[12] Do not turn me over to the desire of my foes,
for false witnesses rise up against me,
spouting malicious accusations.

[13] I remain confident of this:
I will see the goodness of the LORD
in the land of the living.
[14] Wait for the LORD;
be strong and take heart
and wait for the LORD.

Psalm 27 NIV

11 Finding Peace When There Is None

I hate being divorced. I never dreamt the D-word would be a part of my life. I remember the first time I filled out some paperwork after the divorce was final and I had to mark my marital status. The options were single, married, divorced, and widowed. As I checked the *divorced* box, my skin crawled. Reality was sinking in that I had a new identity. After nineteen years, I was no longer a wife, but I didn't get to go back to the *single* box—I had to move forward to the *divorced* box. It was a dagger in my heart.

Sometimes I have trouble calling my ex "my ex." I prefer to refer to him as the father of my kids or the kids' dad. There is something about the words *divorced* and *ex* that just bothers me. I didn't ask for the divorce, and I didn't want the divorce, and so I really dislike all that comes with being divorced.

During the year leading up to our divorce, there was not a lot of yelling and screaming—there were long, levelheaded discussions in the kitchen about finances and the kids and what the future would look like. If you had been a fly on the wall in our house that year, you would have seen their father coming regularly to the house to visit the kids . . . and me. He would lie on the couch while I cooked dinner and talk for hours, or he would lie on the floor and play with the dog while talking with the kids about their day, watching sports, and drinking his sweet tea. Then he would leave.

We went on an overnight family trip to an amusement park. We talked, laughed, and enjoyed ourselves as a family for those two days. We sat in a hot tub at the hotel talking about life—our past, our present, and our future. But it was slowly slipping away . . . two best friends becoming two strangers.

Sometimes I thought we were almost there—like he was coming home. He would stay the night and be emotional about his choice to leave . . . but then inevitably he'd be lured away once again.

And so once the gavel came down in the courtroom, I went to breakfast with my parents and then I returned home, and I threw myself down on my bed and cried my eyes out for two to three hours.

The day after our divorce was final, the kids' dad bought a home a couple states away. He is a pilot, so it was easy for him to come regularly to visit. He had a second home nearby as well, a home he bought one of the times when we were back together after the divorce.

Yes, we got back together . . . after our divorce. While the year leading up to our divorce was the most painful year of my life, it did not hold a candle to how crazy of a roller-coaster ride our family would be on the year *after* our divorce. Oh, friend, I wish I could tell all the stories, but it's best I don't.

The six weeks following our divorce were a blur. The kids' father was away in another state, and Christmas was coming, and he planned to return for Christmas. We celebrated that morning together, the four of us, and he stayed for a long time as the morning turned into afternoon. We had cinnamon rolls and played a family game, and then he helped me out around the house with things that needed to be fixed, and we began to talk.

Talks of reconciliation and remarriage began.

By February, he had moved back home and was sleeping in our finished basement.

You know that feeling when you are on the first hill of a roller coaster—a super steep one, and it's clicking as you go up . . . yeah—that's how I felt. I wanted reconciliation, but I was scared.

Over the next seven weeks, we went to a counselor for the first time together, we met with my parents one-on-one to discuss our reconciliation, he came to a family get-together and was welcomed back, we attended a new church together as a family, we looked at a new home and purchased it to start over again, and then he invited me and the kids to go on a spring break trip to his other new home a few states away.

After a long flight and then a three-hour drive into the desert, we finally arrived at his new home. My brain was struggling to process what I was experiencing. I put on a brave face for the kids and tried to go with the flow, but I was disoriented by seeing this new life he was living with someone else.

This was the part where the roller coaster was at the top of the hill, and we were flying down the other side. You only have one life to live, so figuratively I put my hands up and decided to embrace the moment and enjoy the ride.

We had a great week together. As the week went on, I began to love his new place. The sunny weather was beautiful. The stars at night were amazing. The very small town was interesting. His new friends were nice. I experienced some adventures I had never experienced in my lifetime, and my time with the Lord there was amazing.

But now here is where the roller coaster began to twist and turn.

Something was still off with us. By God's grace, in the most bizarre way, a discovery was made, and it was evident his heart was further from reconciliation than I had hoped.

Now we were upside down on the roller coaster, and I wanted out.

And so we flew home—just me and the kids. For a few weeks there was confusion on his end, as he was torn between two worlds and two women. And then the phone call came. The roller-coaster ride came to a screeching halt, and this is where we both got off the ride.

I was devastated again.

How did I let this happen again?

Am I too much?

Am I not enough?

Why are you not answering my prayers, Lord?

My children! What about my children? I was not just fighting for me—I was fighting for them too.

I had done absolutely everything I believed I could to reconcile. I was emotionally, physically, and spiritually exhausted. There was literally nothing left in me to give. And so with no regrets, I moved forward with letting him go, and everything we had built for nineteen years of marriage and four years of dating began to slip away.

The tearing of one flesh into two was excruciating. It is not God's design for marriage. Marriage is a covenant meant to be kept until death. And when my marriage prematurely ended, I suffered the pain of a death.

Only we were still alive.

And I had no clue how to live the abundant life that Jesus promises while my heart felt ripped in two. But then it happened . . . time passed. During that time, I saturated myself in God's Word. I worked on controlling my thought life, and I prayed my heart out. I drew near to encouragers and compassionate people who were willing to take the time to help me heal. I bought a slew of books and worked my way through them.

And *only* by God's grace am I still standing.

But I have been through the valley of the shadow of death (Psalm 23:4). My journals from that time are overflowing with thoughts of living in the light while wrestling with the dark. The years since have been riddled with me seeking peace over and over when there is none.

I Have So Much Baggage

My greatest fear after the divorce was final was for my children and their future. I had been a homeschooling mom for seven years, and going through a divorce with the kids in the home felt unhealthy. I was concerned.

I had heard someone say, regarding single moms, that as long as your children have one stable parent in the home, they will be okay. So that became one of my life goals: to be the stable parent. But I had a very real problem that did not exist before the divorce—I had some serious baggage.

When I was in college, every Christmas break I stuffed three weeks' worth of clothes into a suitcase that was meant to hold one week's worth of clothes. Then I would wrestle the zipper shut and head out onto the city streets of Chicago.

Now, this was over twenty-five years ago, and the wheels on suitcases were not made quite as well as they are now. My suitcase had four tiny wheels on the long side of the suitcase, and it did not have one of those tall extendable handles. I had to bend down and roll it carefully, as it threatened to tip with every crack and crevice of the sidewalk. I managed to get my very heavy suitcase to the staircase of the subway station. Then I had to drag it down the stairs without it dragging me down the stairs and get through the turnstile, which was super awkward.

Once I was on the subway, I sat down and took a deep breath as I rode to the Chicago O'Hare airport.

When I arrived at the airport, I was not done yet. There were super long corridors, and I dragged that bag all the way to check-in. By the time I got there, I was a hot mess.

Some of us are living life like this. We have past hurts, wounds, and regrets that weigh us down. We may have financial struggles or struggles with our kids, and we are trying to keep it all zipped tight so none of it comes spilling out or knocks us down. We feel like a hot mess.

This is not the life that God wants for us! I'm reminded of Saul when he was being appointed as the first king of Israel. In 1 Samuel we read, "[Kish] had a son whose name was Saul, a handsome young man. There was not a man among the people of Israel more handsome than he. From his shoulders upward he was taller than any of the people" (1 Samuel 9:2). Saul was young, tall, and more handsome than any other man in Israel. He had everything going for him, but guess what he did when he was about to be announced before the people as king?

He hid in the baggage.

> But when they sought him, he could not be found. So they inquired again of the Lord, "Is there a man still to come?" and the Lord said, "Behold, he has hidden himself among the baggage." Then they ran and took him from there. And when he stood among the people, he was taller than any of the people from his shoulders upward.
>
> 1 Samuel 10:21–23

I don't know why Saul hid, but he was clearly scared, and Samuel did not allow him to hide. He pulled him out before the people, and then the people shouted, "Long live the king!" (1 Samuel 10:24). I am sure that he loved that. But there are always naysayers, and in verse 27 it says some of the men said, "How can this man save us?" and despised him.

You see, some people thought he was unqualified. They did not think that he would be a very good king, but Samuel pulled him out and said God wanted to use him. It's the same for you. God wants to use you even though you may feel unqualified. The enemy wants you to hide in the darkness of your baggage, but God wants you to step out into the light so he can use you for his glory.

Step out!

You are not alone. You see, we all have baggage and heavy burdens to bear, but we are just sheep. Sheep are not burden-carrying animals. Donkeys carry burdens, but we are sheep, and that is why our shepherd tells us in Matthew 11:28 (NIV), "Come to me, all you who are weary and burdened, and I will give you rest."

Give It to Jesus

Are you tired of trying to manage all your baggage? It's a lot of work to try to keep it from popping open and being exposed. It's a lot of work to keep it from knocking you down in life. The enemy would love to burden you so you can't move forward. Don't let him win. Give it to Jesus.

You see, when I was walking on the streets of Chicago, I did not have anyone to help me. But if my father had been there and had offered to carry my bag for me, I would have happily passed it over and walked freely.

Jesus Offers Freedom, Peace, and Rest

When I arrived home from the desert after staying with the kids' father for a week, I had an impossibly heavy bag to carry.

My emotions were everywhere, and the enemy tempted me to hide and beat myself up. No way could I carry everything that was happening in my life alone. I needed help. I had to give it to Jesus.

Let's revisit the newly crowned King Saul for a moment. At the end of 1 Samuel 10, after the people shouted "Long live the king!" and others said he wasn't qualified, it says in verse 27 that "he held his peace."

Saul held his peace.

He did not hold on to the cheers, and he did not hold on to the jeers. He held his peace. He stepped out and owned his calling. It takes great strength not to listen to the naysayers around us. It takes great strength to choose peace. Like Saul, we need to stand in the place God has called us to and not be ashamed that our baggage is a part of our story.

Everyone Has Baggage

When you are at the airport in the baggage claim area, it is very clear that not only do we all have baggage but a lot of us have the same bags. More than half the suitcases are black. I happen to have a red bag, so when it shows up on the conveyer belt it is obvious. It makes me smile when I see someone else with a red bag too. I think, *I like that girl!*

All of us have baggage, and many of us have the same bags. The enemy likes to isolate us and make us think we are alone. We are not. Many of us have the same struggles in life, and so we should not be afraid to be open about those struggles. Some of us have very unique baggage from the things we have been through, but if we look hard enough, we will find others who have a similar bag too. It doesn't matter if your baggage is big or small or red or black, Jesus wants to carry your load for you.

Is the load you are carrying today too heavy? Give it to Jesus. Let him carry it for you, and choose peace even when there isn't any.

> Come to me, all you who are weary and burdened, and I will give you rest. Take my yoke upon you and learn from me, for I am gentle and humble in heart, and you will find rest for your souls. For my yoke is easy and my burden is light.
>
> Matthew 11:28–30 NIV

Ten Verses for Finding Peace When There Is None

1) *Remember, the Lord is near.*

The LORD is near to the brokenhearted and saves the crushed in spirit.

Psalm 34:18

2) *Keep your mind focused on trusting in the Lord.*

You keep him in perfect peace whose mind is stayed on you, because he trusts in you.

Isaiah 26:3

3) *You are in a spiritual battle—be strong in the Lord!*

Be strong in the Lord and in the strength of his might.

Ephesians 6:10

4) *You are not alone.*

It is the LORD who goes before you. He will be with you; he will not leave you or forsake you. Do not fear or be dismayed.

Deuteronomy 31:8

5) *Give your worries to Jesus.*

Casting all your anxieties on him, because he cares for you.

1 Peter 5:7

6) ***Run to Jesus and rest in him.***

Come to me, all who labor and are heavy laden, and I will give you rest. Take my yoke upon you, and learn from me, for I am gentle and lowly in heart, and you will find rest for your souls. For my yoke is easy, and my burden is light.

Matthew 11:28–30

7) ***Keep believing. Cling to hope.***

May the God of hope fill you with all joy and peace in believing, so that by the power of the Holy Spirit you may abound in hope.

Romans 15:13

8) ***This is unnatural, but rejoice.***

We rejoice in our sufferings, knowing that suffering produces endurance, and endurance produces character, and character produces hope.

Romans 5:3–4

9) ***Peace is only found in Jesus.***

I have said these things to you, that in me you may have peace. In the world you will have tribulation. But take heart; I have overcome the world.

John 16:33

10) ***God is present with you. Let him be your refuge and strength.***

God is our refuge and strength, a very present help in trouble.

Psalm 46:1

REFLECTION QUESTIONS

1. What does your baggage look like? Do you struggle with baggage from the past? What burdens are you carrying right now?

2. Saul had everything going for him. He was young, tall, and handsome, and yet he was scared to step into his anointing as king. In what ways has the enemy used some of your baggage to make you fear or hide?

3. Read Matthew 11:28–30. What does Jesus say you will find when you take your burdens to him?

4. Go to Jesus now in prayer and give him your burdens. Write your prayer out as you exchange your weariness for his peace and rest.

5. Who do you know who has similar baggage to you? How can you be an encouragement to them as they try to carry their heavy bags?

12 Finding Strength When You Feel Tired

When I was a young wife, one of my favorite passages of Scripture to study was Proverbs chapter 31. Proverbs 31 was written by a mother to her son. She went through the alphabet one letter at a time, giving him attributes that he was to seek out in his future wife. I studied all those attributes one by one because I desired to become like the woman described in Proverbs 31.

I wanted to be a great wife! The Proverbs 31 woman feared God. She was known for her kindness. She rose early to care for her family. She worked hard, and she was a treasure to her husband. I wanted to be her.

Later in Proverbs 31 it says, "Her children arise and call her blessed; her husband also, and he praises her: 'Many women do noble things, but you surpass them all'" (vv. 28–29 NIV). When my husband left me, suddenly these verses hurt my soul. I no longer had a husband, so how could I fulfill my dream to become a Proverbs 31 woman? I certainly had not *surpassed them all*, since he had chosen another woman over me.

Verse 10 of Proverbs 31 says that "a wife of noble character" is "worth far more than rubies." But the man I loved with all my heart, who'd given me the title of wife, had just removed that title. The darkness began to push in. I was left to question my worth. I certainly wasn't worth far more than rubies to my husband.

I wrestled with the fact that there was no possible way for me to be a Proverbs 31 woman without a husband, and so I let that dream go, and I asked God, *Where do I go from here?* And then I began waiting on his answer.

One day I was in a store, and I saw a plaque with Proverbs 31:25 (NLT) on it: "She is clothed with strength and dignity, and she laughs without fear of the future." I stopped in my tracks. God's light began to shine into my darkness, and I thought, *That's the woman I want to be.*

Strong.

Dignified.

Laughing.

No fear.

I want to be remembered as a woman with a light heart, who smiled and laughed easily because she was not worried about all the details of life and instead was resting in her Savior's love. And so I put that plaque in my cart and went straight to the register and bought it. There was this empty spot on my bedroom wall with an old nail hole, and I grabbed a nail, stuck it in the hole, and then hung the plaque on my bedroom wall right where my wedding photo once was. Then I changed the entire color scheme of my bedroom to match my new plaque.

It felt good. It felt hopeful. I was getting stronger. I continued with this theme. In my home office, I hung a chalkboard, and I wrote Proverbs 31:25 on the chalkboard and made it my theme verse for that year. There before me, every day, the qualities I wanted to live out in my life hung as a reminder in both my bedroom and my office.

I Want to Be Clothed Like the Proverbs 31 Woman

When Christ died on the cross, he offered us salvation through the covering of our sin with his blood. God has clothed us in his righteousness. But the Proverbs 31 woman was not only clothed in the blood of Christ, but she was clothed with something more. What was the Proverbs 31 woman clothed with? "She is clothed with strength and dignity, and she laughs without fear of the future" (Proverbs 31:25 NLT).

1) *Strength*

A Proverbs 31 woman is clothed with strength. When I think of a strong woman, I think of a woman who can withstand great pressure both mentally and emotionally. She has courage in the face of her fears. Her confidence is not in herself, but rather it comes from the God she serves. She can be gracious in the midst of hostility, she is willing to make great sacrifices and deny herself for the sake of her children, and she does not compromise her principles in the face of temptation. She is strong.

2) *Dignity*

A Proverbs 31 woman knows her worth and acts accordingly. When I think of a woman who is dignified, I think of a woman who is composed and who acts honorably. Her actions match her words, she is not caught up in sin, and she takes the high road yet is not too proud to be at the lowest position. She is humble. She is willing to do hard work, knowing there is a payoff later, and she has great confidence and peace that is seen by those around her. She is decent to those around her and respectable. She is dignified.

3) Laughter

The Proverbs 31 woman laughs with ease. When I think of a woman who laughs with ease, I think of a woman who is secure. She has no fear of the future because she is a woman at peace and has rest in her soul. She is not wringing her hands or losing sleep over her troubles. She is not worrying because she is trusting in God to take care of her here on earth, and her eternity is secure in heaven. She is free to be happy and enjoy life.

She is strong, she is dignified, and she laughs with no fear of the future.

Strong. Dignified. Secure.

It does not matter if I'm married or single, I want to be this type of woman!

Do you struggle with being strong, dignified, and secure? Maybe you have a fear of failure or of being rejected or saying something stupid, of not being good enough, pretty enough, organized enough, or just plain *enough*. Me too. Our confidence must not be in ourselves. We are weak, but God is strong.

Clothing covers our nakedness. It protects us from being exposed. We need to put on the Proverbs 31 woman's clothes. You see, when we take our eyes off ourselves and put them on our amazing God, our confidence changes. Our confidence is no longer in ourselves but rather in our creator. He is the one who laid the earth's foundations, put the stars in the sky, commands the sun to rise each day, holds the storehouses of snow, tells the lightning when to strike—and he loves you.

Let him clothe you in his strength.

But I'm So Broken

It's awfully hard to walk around with strength, dignity, and a smile on your face when you are broken and everyone sees it.

I know. But have you ever heard this phrase? *You can't use an egg unless it's broken.*

It's true! I love eggs! I eat two almost every day for breakfast. Eggs are useless until they are broken. Once they are broken, they have so many uses. You can scramble them, boil them, put them in your fried rice, or make chocolate chip cookies with them. A broken egg isn't pretty, but once it is put to good use, it is wonderful.

Is something in your life broken?

The enemy would love to keep you stuck in your brokenness, but I have a feeling God has a plan to use that very area that you want to hide. God wants to use your brokenness. Perhaps you have a broken relationship, a past failure, or a current struggle you cannot overcome. Perhaps you have prayed for relief and feel like God is not hearing your prayers.

Jesus said, "In this world you will have trouble" (John 16:33 NIV). This is a promise. Life is hard. We all face troubles of many kinds. Let's look at this promise in its context: "I have told you these things, so that in me you may have peace. In this world you will have trouble. But take heart! I have overcome the world" (John 16:33 NIV).

Jesus told us we will have trouble *so that* we would have peace in him, *so that* we would take heart, and *so that* we would remember that he has overcome the world.

Sometimes we can be surprised by how hard life is and begin to doubt that God cares. The enemy wants to keep you stuck in doubt, but Jesus told us we would have trouble. So do not be surprised—instead, be strong.

Friend, your brokenness can even make you stronger.

Your brokenness can free you to be more used by God than before you went through that hard thing. You see, your brokenness has made you less self-sufficient and more dependent on God. It has made you more compassionate and understanding of the hard things that others go through in life. And it has made you pray more and seek God more than you ever would have without that hard thing.

Let the Lord Renew Your Strength

It can be exhausting trying to be strong day in and day out. There are days when I am just plain tired of being strong. Then I'm reminded of Isaiah 40:31 (NIV), which says, "Those who hope in the LORD will renew their strength. They will soar on wings like eagles; they will run and not grow weary, they will walk and not be faint."

Take it one day at a time. Just for today, put your hope in the Lord. And then tomorrow, do that again. Every day repeat your hope in the Lord.

If we will just be patient and wait on him, he will renew our strength and help us to walk, run, and even soar through life with strength, dignity, and no fear. Keep trusting him with the reins of your life, and keep walking with the King.

Ten Verses for When You Feel Tired

1) Spend time in God's Word. He will give you strength.

My soul melts away for sorrow; strengthen me according to your word!

Psalm 119:28

2) God desires to give you rest. Friend—God gives you permission to rest. Seek rest and seek God during that rest and trust in him.

Come to me, all who labor and are heavy laden, and I will give you rest. Take my yoke upon you, and learn from me, for I am gentle and lowly in heart, and you will find rest for your souls. For my yoke is easy, and my burden is light.

Matthew 11:28–30

3) ***God provides all that you need at all times. He will sustain you.***

He said to me, "My grace is sufficient for you, for my power is made perfect in weakness." Therefore I will boast all the more gladly of my weaknesses, so that the power of Christ may rest upon me.

2 Corinthians 12:9

4) ***God will use this trial in your life for your good and his glory.***

We know that for those who love God all things work together for good, for those who are called according to his purpose.

Romans 8:28

5) ***Is part of your weariness due to wounding from others? God knows your brokenness, and he promises to heal you and restore you if you will release it to him.***

He heals the brokenhearted and binds up their wounds.

Psalm 147:3

6) ***Continue to do good and serve him. Do not give up!***

Let us not grow weary of doing good, for in due season we will reap, if we do not give up.

Galatians 6:9

7) ***Give thanks to God that he provides strength in your times of need.***

My flesh and my heart may fail, but God is the strength of my heart and my portion forever.

Psalm 73:26

8) ***Sleep well. God has it all under control.***

In peace I will both lie down and sleep; for you alone, O Lord, make me dwell in safety.

Psalm 4:8

9) Be still and wait for the Lord. He is at work even when we cannot see him, and he has a purpose for your trials.

Even youths shall faint and be weary, and young men shall fall exhausted; but they who wait for the Lord shall renew their strength; they shall mount up with wings like eagles; they shall run and not be weary; they shall walk and not faint.

Isaiah 40:30–31

10) Seek him earnestly! Spend quality time with God in his Word and in prayer.

O God, you are my God; earnestly I seek you; my soul thirsts for you; my flesh faints for you, as in a dry and weary land where there is no water. So I have looked upon you in the sanctuary, beholding your power and glory. Because your steadfast love is better than life, my lips will praise you.

Psalm 63:1–3

REFLECTION QUESTIONS

1. All of us, whether we are married or single, can be clothed like the Proverbs 31 woman. Look at her three pieces of clothing: strength, dignity, and laughter. Which one of these describes you most, and why? Which one of these describes you least, and why?

2. In what area of your life do you feel broken? In what ways has the enemy used your brokenness to get in the way of you living your life with strength, dignity, and laughter?

3. Read John 16:33. What does Jesus say we will all face in our lives? As a result, what is his instruction to us?

4. Look at Isaiah 40:31. What is the key to renewing our strength in the Lord? How can you live this out in your life this week to help you overcome your weariness?

5. Pray Proverbs 31:25 over your life. Write your prayer out. Now think of a family member or friend who needs prayer, and pray this verse over their life as well. Let them know you are praying for them today.

13 Finding Contentment with the Woman in the Mirror

I've always had long stick-straight hair. When I was a little girl, my sisters and I would take turns on Saturday nights sitting in front of my mom while she rolled our hair in pink sponge rollers. Oh how I loved waking up on Sunday mornings with the most beautiful curls! As we headed out the door to church, I always felt pretty.

Then I became a teenager, and like most teenagers in the 80s, I wanted to get a perm. So every few months my grandmother would roll my hair in very tiny rollers and put a solution on my hair that made the curl permanent for a few months. After she took my rollers out, she dried and fluffed my hair, and it was wavy and beautiful! It felt so good to have my straight hair permanently curly—no rollers needed!

Then in college straight hair came into style. Humph. I had never felt pretty with my straight hair, so how was I going to pull this look off? I couldn't do it. I only felt pretty when my hair was curled, so I just kept curling my hair with a curling iron, trying to do a straighter wavy look but always feeling a little dissatisfied with my hair.

Beauty. The enemy knows that in the heart of every woman is a longing and desire to be beautiful. God created beauty. He himself is beautiful, and his creation is beautiful. He created beautiful sunsets, waterfalls, peacocks, leaves that change colors in the fall, snow that sparkles in the winter, and spring flowers that bloom. There is no end to God's glory displayed in creation.

Genesis 1:27 tells us we were made in God's image: "So God created man in his own image, in the image of God he created him; male and female he created them." It makes sense that the enemy would come after the image bearers of God. It was Eve he went after first in the garden of Eden, not Adam. And when he comes after women today, I believe he strikes hard in the area of our beauty. It is a vulnerable area for most of us. It seems as soon as we achieve some sort of contentment, our cycle changes, a few pounds are gained, a blemish or sunspot shows up, a new diet becomes all the rage, a new fashion trend makes us feel out of style, or we move into menopause and our body begins changing in ways we cannot control.

Is it wrong to desire beauty? The Bible says Queen Esther was simply stunning. God used her beauty to help her to be picked by the king. But what I love even more about Esther is she was brave, humble, sacrificial, and beautiful on the inside.

Inner beauty. It truly is what matters, but the enemy wants us to believe it's a consolation prize. He wants us to strive for an unattainable goal and be dissastisfied with who God made us to be. The enemy wants to make us feel like hiding in darkness. He does not want us to be women who stand confident in who God made us to be and fearless as we step into God's purpose for our lives.

But we all have insecurities. Some of us more than others. When I linger in front of the mirror for a moment, what do I see? A gray hair popping out, two big sunspots on my cheek, and bags under my eyes. Then there's my muffin top—possibly the thing that makes me most insecure. For me, all it takes is a mirror to make me very discontent.

Proverbs 20:29 says, "The glory of young men is their strength, but the splendor of old men is their gray hair." Gray hair—it's a sign of aging, and it's a hard one for me. Life was easier before gray hairs. The older I get, the grayer my hair becomes and the more work it is to try to cover them. And yet, Proverbs 16:31 says, "Gray hair is a crown of glory; it is gained in a righteous life." God sees gray hair as a splendor and crown of glory, not because gray hair is more righteous than nongray hair, but because there is wisdom and knowledge gained through aging and experiencing the many seasons of life.

I don't know if you are young or old or if you have gray hairs or not, but in our culture, most signs of aging are viewed as negative. In God's economy, the signs of aging you see in the mirror are a sign of maturity. It is a sign that we have learned some life lessons that the young have yet to learn. It should be a badge of honor, or as his Word says, a "crown of glory."

Though we all may face the darkness of discontentment with our bodies, God promises to be faithful. "Even to your old age I am he, and to gray hairs I will carry you" (Isaiah 46:4). Those who are in their golden years can testify that God is faithful. Through every twist and turn of life, they have experienced the goodness of God. Oh, what great value our elderly have to the church to bring wisdom and knowledge and experience that the young simply do not have. We must not marginalize the elderly in our churches. And to my dear older friends, if you are in your golden years, you have great value to God. He sees you, and the same God who carried you in your youth will continue to carry you into old age.

The Power of Comparison

When we look in the mirror, our inner critic can get out of control. The only thing worse than a mirror is comparison. We all do it.

We compare ourselves to:

1. Ourselves and our pre-baby days

   I marvel at pictures of myself from high school and college. I wonder why in the world I felt fat back then because I was not fat at all. I only wish I could be that thin again!
2. Our siblings

   Since fifth grade, I have been the curvy sister. Moderation has not always been easy for me, and I've been on every diet you can imagine and am currently on one right now. For most of my adult life, both of my sisters have naturally been slender; need I say more?!
3. Our friends

   Oh to have long legs! I have some beautiful tall friends who make me feel short (you know who you are!). Those who know me well know I always have a heel on unless I am exercising. Even my flip-flops have a heel (in case you wonder, I'm 5′2″).
4. Our foes

   I'll admit I've compared myself to the *other woman*. I won't explain where she has me beat, but there is one area where I compare myself and fall short, and it's annoying. It's also important to remember that if comparison with our friends turns into jealousy, then we are way off track from where God wants us to be and have gone from being a friend to a foe. Jealousy is ugly and deadly. It ruins friendships! Do not do it. It'd be better to pluck our eye out (Mark 9:47) than to covet our neighbor's beauty.

5. Strangers

   Yes, I'm guilty of this one too. I've walked through the mall and seen beautiful women my own age who are thin, tan, have shiny hair and glowing skin, and I'm floored. How do they do that?
6. Celebrities

   Comparing yourself to celebrities is a lose-lose situation. They have trainers, chefs, nannies, hairstylists, fashion designers, and airbrushing! We can't possibly keep up.

Discontentment with the woman in the mirror is a never-ending merry-go-round that the enemy uses to steal our joy. We go around and around trying to get off, and though we might be able to disembark for a moment, we somehow end up back on the miserable ride once again.

So what do we do with all this comparison that feels almost natural?

It's a matter of mindset. The enemy is attacking our minds! He wants us to doubt that God is good. He wants me to wonder why God did not give me what some other women have, and he wants you to feel the same way. I refuse to let the enemy control me with my insecurities! Contentment is being satisfied and at peace with what you have and who you are.

So think for a moment. What is it you don't like about yourself? Name it. Now, praise God for it. Go ahead—do it.

Does it feel strange?

Here's an example of my prayer of praise:

Dear Heavenly Father,

Thank you for my muffin top—it means I've had an abundance of food. Thank you for my gray hairs—it means I've been blessed with many years of life. Thank you for my bags under my eyes—it means I have been blessed with many people in my home to love and care for and a thriving ministry online. Thank you for my sunspot—it reminds me of all those fun days on the beach and at the pool. Thank you for giving me so many years to be alive that I now have gray hairs. And thank you for loving me so much that you died on the cross for me. I love you, Jesus. It's in your name I pray, Amen.

That's a strange prayer, isn't it? The world says to suck the muffin top in, color the gray hairs, conceal the bags, have the sunspot removed, and on it goes.

It's hard to praise God for something that drives you nuts, I know. That's because you've been focusing on it and thinking so negatively for so long that your mind can barely consider the idea of actually praising God for how you are made. You have been beating yourself up with comparison!

Dear God, "I praise you, for I am fearfully and wonderfully made. Wonderful are your works; my soul knows it very well" (Psalm 139:14).

Focus on the wonderful things he has given you—eyes to see, ears to hear, hands to serve, feet that walk, a heart that beats, lungs that hold air, a brain that can read and understand this book, and a heart to feel God's love and love others. Wow! You are amazing. God made you, and he says you were wonderfully made! Trust him that he made you the way you are for his purpose and glory!

Proverbs 31:30 says, "Charm is deceitful, and beauty is vain, but a woman who fears the Lord is to be praised." God says beauty is vain. It is fleeting. No one is going to outrun old age unless they have an early death. Whether we like it or not, even the most beautiful woman in the world will eventually grow so old that no amount of plastic surgery can correct the weakness of her bones, her hearing, her eyesight, the wrinkling of her skin, the spots that appear on her hands, or the arthritis, dementia, and frailness that set in.

The bottom line is this—the enemy does not want you to be content. He hates you, and he wants you to hate yourself and your creator as well. "But godliness with contentment is great gain" (1 Timothy 6:6 NIV). If the enemy has gained ground and knocked you down in this area, it's time to get up. Fight for contentment. The fight for contentment is a fight to see. It is a fight to see things from God's perspective rather than the world's perspective.

Insecurity Starts Young

Do you remember the first time you realized you were different or had a flaw that you didn't like? I was in third grade when I realized I had a serious problem.

I knew I had a speech impediment because kids on the school bus had pointed it out, but it hadn't really bothered me much . . . until the day speech therapy began. I had trouble pronouncing the letters *s* and *z*. For some reason, I said them out of the side of my mouth. This was not good.

A couple times a week in my public school, I left my class and friends and headed to the speech therapy room, where I wore headphones and repeated over and over the *s* and *z* sounds correctly. My speech therapist was kind. We played games, and I repeated "Sally sold seashells down by the seashore" until I got it right. I practiced at home, I practiced at therapy, and a few long years later—voilà! No more impediment!

But then a new issue arose. I was a cheerleader, and I guess I had weak vocal cords because I regularly lost my voice after games. As my coach said, if I had yelled properly from my diaphragm, I would not have lost my voice so much. So I tried harder to cheer properly, but all the way through high school my vocal cords were always strained.

Losing my voice became a regular occurrence in my life into adulthood. When I got a cold, it went straight to my throat, and I would lose my voice easily—and when I say I lost my voice, I mean it was gone and not a squeak would come out. I was silent for about five days while tea and honey became my best friend.

If you've watched my YouTube videos, you'll hear me occasionally reference having a cold and losing my voice. It still happens, just not as frequently as when I was a kid.

The week of my appearance on the nationally syndicated *Rachael Ray Show*, I lost my voice. There were about five days between the camera crews coming to my house and my flight to New York City. When the camera crews came I was fine, but the very next day I lost my voice. I prayed so hard that the Lord would return my voice so I could be on the show.

Do you see the irony in the fact that the very thing I love to do—speak—is the very area, physically, I am weak in? God has humbled me in this area. I mean really, I couldn't talk straight as a kid, and when I finally could say my *s*'s correctly, I started losing my voice!

God has kept me dependent on him to have a voice. I am sure that this weakness is God's way of keeping me at his feet in prayer, remembering he is the one who has given me my voice and he could easily take it away. My voice is his.

I am reminded of Moses in Exodus 4:10–12 (emphasis added):

> But Moses said to the Lord, "Oh, my Lord, I am not eloquent, either in the past or since you have spoken to your servant, but *I am slow of speech and of tongue.*" Then the Lord said to him, "*Who has made man's mouth?* Who makes him mute, or deaf, or seeing, or blind? *Is it not I, the Lord? Now therefore go, and I will be with your mouth and teach you what you shall speak.*"

Moses responded, "Oh, my Lord, please send someone else" (Exodus 4:13). He doubted himself and his abilities. While it's good to be humble, to be filled with self-doubt to the point of not following God is sin.

When I was in my midtwenties, I really feared trying to lead because I felt like others saw me as too young and immature. While this didn't stop me from leading, I had a lot of insecurities I wrestled with from the start of doing ministry, and I clung to 1 Timothy 4:12 (NIV): "Don't let anyone look down on you because you are young, but set an example for the believers in speech, in conduct, in love, in faith and in purity."

Do your insecurities keep you from wanting to step up and serve God?

The enemy wants to hold you down. He wants you to feel like you are not enough. Not good enough. Not smart enough. Not pretty enough. Not eloquent enough. Not organized enough. He wants to keep you hidden in the shadows.

God does not look at the outward appearance, birth order, or background. Often he chooses the overlooked of this world to lead. In a culture where the younger served the older, Isaac, Jacob, Joseph, Moses, and David were all the youngest in their families, and they served God mightily.

Contentment Is an Inside Job

God created you on purpose. Before you ever took a breath, Psalm 139 tells us that God was creating you in your mother's womb. He not only created your body, but he created your mind as well. It is in our mind that we must learn contentment with our bodies and our limitations. We must challenge the thoughts and the lies that come at us from both the enemy and from inside our mind.

This is an inside job.

No one else can do this for us. No one else can praise us enough or make us feel beautiful enough to take away our deep need for contentment. No one else can rewind time and undo the terrible words that bullies, siblings, parents, teachers, coaches, or even friends have said to us. And it's tempting to go about fixing our insecurities in all the wrong ways.

- It's tempting to become a perfectionist to avoid criticism, but taken too far, perfectionism can lead to being stuck, obsessing over small things, and never feeling good enough because no one is perfect.
- It's tempting to try to prove our worth by chasing success, but in the end, it only leads to a successful insecure person. Sometimes those who act as if they are better than others are the most insecure people in the room.
- It's tempting to serve, help, and sacrifice for others just so you feel needed, desired, and loved. In the end, you may just end up feeling burned out and underappreciated and no more content than the day you started living that way.
- It's tempting to decide we are going to be confident in ourselves and put up boundaries to protect ourselves so others cannot affect us at all. But taken too far, we can end up selfish, stubborn, and alone.

We must be wise.

We must be aware of the enemy's schemes.

We must not try to fix our insecurities apart from God.

While we can't control all the ways that this world will bombard us, we can control our response. God wants us to stand in his light and believe him when he says we are wonderfully made. He wants us to stand in his light and believe him when he says that godliness with contentment is great gain. He wants us to stand in his light and believe him when he says he loved us so much that even while we were sinners, he died for us.

Rest in his goodness.
Live loved.
And be kind to that woman in the mirror.

Ten Verses for Finding Contentment with the Woman in the Mirror

1) *God created you. Be thankful for how wonderfully he made you and what he has given you.*

For you formed my inward parts; you knitted me together in my mother's womb. I praise you, for I am fearfully and wonderfully made. Wonderful are your works; my soul knows it very well.

Psalm 139:13–14

2) *You were created in the image of God. Isn't that humbling and amazing to think about?*

So God created man in his own image, in the image of God he created him; male and female he created them.

Genesis 1:27

3) *God is looking at your heart, not your outward appearance.*

For the Lord sees not as man sees: man looks on the outward appearance, but the Lord looks on the heart.

1 Samuel 16:7

4) *God is concerned with our bodies. He gave them to us to steward.*

Do you not know that your body is a temple of the Holy Spirit within you, whom you have from God? You are not your own, for you were bought with a price. So glorify God in your body.

1 Corinthians 6:19–20

5) ***Don't allow your body image to get you sidetracked from your real goals in life—including the imperishable beauty of a gentle and quiet spirit.***

Do not let your adorning be external—the braiding of hair and the putting on of gold jewelry, or the clothing you wear—but let your adorning be the hidden person of the heart with the imperishable beauty of a gentle and quiet spirit, which in God's sight is very precious.

1 Peter 3:3–4

6) ***Another goal is to fear the Lord. This means to have a sense of awe of God and to appreciate his character and his holiness.***

Charm is deceitful, and beauty is vain, but a woman who fears the LORD is to be praised.

Proverbs 31:30

7) ***Are you training for godliness? Godliness is revealed in someone who is so focused on God that their conduct and character reflect their private, intimate walk with God.***

Train yourself for godliness; for while bodily training is of some value, godliness is of value in every way, as it holds promise for the present life and also for the life to come.

1 Timothy 4:7–8

8) ***Obsessing over every little bite we take and worrying that we might gain a pound keep us from appreciating the gift of food that God has given us. But likewise, indulging in food to the point of gluttony is abusing the gift of food. In the middle is self-control, balance, and freedom.***

So, whether you eat or drink, or whatever you do, do all to the glory of God.

1 Corinthians 10:31

9) God created you for good works. You have to find the place where you are free, and it is not a number on the scale or a certain dress size. It's when you are eating right and getting proper rest and exercise.

For we are his workmanship, created in Christ Jesus for good works, which God prepared beforehand, that we should walk in them.

Ephesians 2:10

10) You are not alone, and because God is with you, you never have to live in fear. He will give you strength each and every day.

I can do all things through him who strengthens me.

Philippians 4:13

REFLECTION QUESTIONS

1. In what areas do you struggle with contentment with the woman in the mirror? Think back. At what age did this begin?

2. Do you have a problem with comparing yourself to the old version of yourself or with others? How has the enemy used your insecurities to trip you up in life?

3. Tell of a time when God used one of your weaknesses or flaws to be a blessing to you or others?

4. Contentment is being satisfied and at peace with what you have. Read 1 Timothy 6:6. What should you pursue alongside contentment? What do these two qualities put together give you?

5. Write a prayer thanking God specifically for the ways he made you. List both some of your good qualities and some of the ones you struggle with in your prayer. Now go and be kinder to the woman in the mirror this week.

14 Finding Your Way Forward When You Feel Stuck

There used to be a huge grandfather clock in the foyer of our home. I loved the sound of the chimes striking one, then two, then three, then four, and so on. It was a lovely sound. After the kids' father moved out, the cost of the maintenance of the beautiful clock made me decide to sell it. Once it was gone, the wall was very empty in the foyer, kind of like the other half of my bed, the empty chair at our kitchen table, and that spot in the garage where his car used to be.

I felt stuck. I couldn't change what was happening. I so badly wanted to go backward rather than forward, but that was not an option. It was painful and hard and so incredibly frustrating. I may not have been moving forward, but I was still standing.

And so after the clock was gone, I found the perfect quote to hang on that bare wall. It said:

> "Until God opens the next door
> praise him in the hallway."

And that is exactly what I did. A lot of days, I did not know how to move forward or what to do next, but every day I praised the Lord that I was still standing.

Stuck

Have you ever stood in line at the grocery store, sizing up the other lines? You get into one line, and it seems to be moving very slowly, so you change to a line that appears to be going faster. Then you discover that you would have been better off if you had just stayed in the original line.

The same thing always happens to me on the highway. If there is a slowdown, I will inevitably switch lanes to try to find a faster lane and end up in a slower lane. And in the doctor's waiting room, it's the same. I enter, sign in, look around the waiting room, and take a seat. Often, thirty minutes later I'm still waiting, but everyone else who was in the room when I arrived has already gone in and come out.

Sometimes I just feel plain stuck in life. I try to move forward, but somehow I end up two steps behind. I pray consistently, fervently, relentlessly, and persistently day in and day out with no signs of change. The days drag into months with no change, and this is when the darkness creeps in, tempting me to run away, seek an escape, take a vacation, go on a shopping spree, or eat a carton of ice cream in one sitting.

Not acting on these urges takes wisdom, strength, and discipline. But sometimes I don't feel like I have the strength for another day, and it's in these times I find myself on my knees, crying out to God through tears and begging him to sustain me. Praying that he would give me patience while I wait on him.

But after I get up from my knees and dry my tears, then what? Though my heart is one of dependence and surrender,

I am still stuck. Life is still happening, and to everyone else it looks like I'm moving forward, but really I'm moving forward in darkness and confusion.

Walk with the King

Without a clear direction from God, we can feel lost. When I feel confused and stuck, I like to organize. Perhaps it's a form of trying to get the parts of my life that I can control under control so I can handle everything else that feels out of control. This is a temporary fix because I can't really control much in life.

Paul says in Ephesians 5:15, "Look carefully then how you walk, not as unwise but as wise."

Look how? *Carefully*.

Look at what? *How you walk*.

What are the two ways we can walk forward? *Unwisely or wisely*.

Look. Our eyes are like mini cameras. They are the windows to our life. The structure of the eye is very complex, but it is limited. We can only see physical things, and these physical things are only part of reality. The spiritual realm is *just* as real, but we cannot see it with our physical eyes.

Look carefully. And so Paul says to look carefully. Use your spiritual eyes when you look at life because he says you have two choices. You can either walk as unwise or as wise. We must practice discernment in the way we walk forward. We must learn to discern the will of God in our lives, and the only way we can do that is to know God—know his Word and know his ways. The way we move forward in life may look different from the world. We may not go at the speed of the world, but we are safest when we take our time to walk wisely right in the center of God's will.

Paul goes on in Ephesians 5 to say, "Making the best use of the time, because the days are evil. Therefore do not be foolish, but understand what the will of the Lord is" (Ephesians 5:16–17).

Make the best use of your time. There it is. There's a command for us. Even when we are stuck, God cares about how we spend our time. We are to make the *best* use of our time!

But how do we know what the best use of our time is?

Verse 17 says we can know by *understanding God's will.*

How will we understand God's will?

By walking with the King!

Friend, time management for a Christian begins with your time spent with God. Are you spending time with God every day?

How will you know how to spend your time, what you should commit to, and what you should say no to if you are not in communion with God? We need to understand his will, and that comes through the reading of his Word and prayer.

It can be tempting to pray over our lists, our plans, our wants, and our desires and simply ask God to bless all of it rather than surrender it all to God. The mistake here is that we may put more on our plate than God would ever put on our plate. As a result of having way too much on our plate, our stress levels rise. When our lives are too full, there is no room for sickness or error, and then we can't figure out why life is so hard. We get frustrated with God, and it's not God's fault. Sadly, we do this to ourselves, and God does not want his children stressed out doing a hundred different things each day. He wants us to rest in him. He wants us to make the *best* use of our time.

This goes the opposite way too—maybe you aren't someone who's putting too much on your plate, but maybe instead you just love indulging in life's pleasures. Perhaps you love to waste time scrolling on social media, bingeing on movies, always taking a break, seeking fun only, and trying to escape the hard things of life. As a result, others in the home, workplace, or church have to pick up your slack. This isn't the *best* use of our time either.

Do Not Get Drunk

Paul continues in Ephesians 5 and says, "And do not get drunk with wine, for that is debauchery, but be filled with the Spirit" (v. 18). So here we have an interesting contrast. We have being *drunk with wine* compared to being *filled with the Spirit.*

Friends, feeling stuck in life can drive us to want to drink in excess. You may be tempted to turn to alcohol to relieve your stress or give you some extra help to get you through this hard time. That's the enemy showing up again in the darkness, and Paul says, *don't do it.*

Let the strength you need come from the Holy Spirit.

Let your sadness drive you to Jesus.

Let your stress and pressure drive you to Jesus.

When you celebrate with friends, let it be in genuine joy of the Lord and not just the debauchery that comes from drunkenness.

Debauchery is living without limits or with reckless abandon. It's living life completely out of control.

God has called us to live a life under the control of the Holy Spirit rather than living with reckless abandon and without limits. It might feel like freedom to get drunk temporarily, but in the end, it will hurt you.

We Need God's Help

Do not be troubled by the strange need you feel inside for help. That is normal. God wants that inner need in you to cause you to turn to him and let his Spirit help you and strengthen you.

When you are depending on the Holy Spirit, there will be two things evident in your life. Look at Ephesians 5:19–20:

> Addressing one another in psalms and hymns and spiritual songs, singing and making melody to the Lord with your heart, giving thanks always and for everything to God the Father in the name of our Lord Jesus Christ.

Look at the heart change that comes from being a woman who walks wisely. She will be *singing and making melody to the Lord with her heart*, and she will be *giving thanks!*

Is this what your life looks like today?

Would someone speaking about you say "She is filled with the Spirit, and she walks carefully. She walks wisely. She walks in the will of the Lord"?

Are You Waiting on God, or Is God Waiting on You?

Waiting on God and his will to take place in our lives is good. It is essential as a believer to wait on God and not get ahead of him. But waiting passively for God to do something supernatural is not typically how God works.

Sometimes God is waiting on us to take a step forward in faith and courage, and then and only then do we begin to see the work of God's hand in our lives. Are you wondering if you should be still or move?

Reading God's Word is good. Studying God's Word is good. Memorizing God's Word is good. Seeking God's will in prayer is good. And there is also a time, my friend, when we are to strap on the full armor of God and step into the spiritual battle and actively fight the enemy.

> For we do not wrestle against flesh and blood, but against the rulers, against the authorities, against the cosmic powers over this present darkness, against the spiritual forces of evil in the heavenly places.
>
> Ephesians 6:12

How do you do this?

Repent of your sin.
Love God.
Love your neighbors.
Love your enemies.
Speak truth in love.
Give grace and mercy to others.
Share the gospel.
Push back darkness.
Help others overcome sin in their lives.
Hold on to hope.
Fight for joy.
Keep moving forward.

Remember this: "He who is in you is greater than he who is in the world" (1 John 4:4). The victory is already yours.

> And I heard a loud voice in heaven, saying, "Now the salvation and the power and the kingdom of our God and the authority of his Christ have come, for the accuser of our brothers has been thrown down, who accuses them day and night before our God. And they have conquered him by the blood of the Lamb and by the word of their testimony, for they loved not their lives even unto death. Therefore, rejoice, O heavens and you who dwell in them! But woe to you, O earth and sea, for the devil

has come down to you in great wrath, because he knows that his time is short!"

Revelation 12:10–12

As you move forward, remember this: other people in our lives are never the enemy—Satan is. He is on the move, a roaring lion seeking whom he may devour. Each new morning, may we be courageous women, clothed in the blood of the lamb, ready to fight our enemy through the power of Jesus as we push back darkness and stand in the light. Keep on going.

Ten Verses for When You Feel Stuck

1) ***We aren't going backward. We are going forward. Don't let the past hold you back.***

But one thing I do: forgetting what lies behind and straining forward to what lies ahead, I press on toward the goal for the prize of the upward call of God in Christ Jesus.

Philippians 3:13–14

2) ***Fully trust and surrender to God during this time. Wait quietly on the Lord.***

The LORD is good to those who wait for him, to the soul who seeks him.

Lamentations 3:25

3) ***Even though we don't know the future, we can still have hope. God is deepening our faith during this season of waiting.***

Hope that is seen is not hope. For who hopes for what he sees? But if we hope for what we do not see, we wait for it with patience.

Romans 8:24–25

4) ***As you wait for him, God will provide you with all the strength you need.***

Have you not known? Have you not heard? The LORD is the everlasting God, the Creator of the ends of the earth. He does not faint or grow weary; his understanding is unsearchable. He gives power to the faint, and to him who has no might he increases strength.

Isaiah 40:28–29

5) ***Jesus is a steady, secure, strong foundation, and anything we build with him will last forever. When our lives are built on his sure promises, we have no reason to fear.***

Our soul waits for the LORD; he is our help and our shield. For our heart is glad in him, because we trust in his holy name. Let your steadfast love, O LORD, be upon us, even as we hope in you.

Psalm 33:20–22

6) ***Be strong and courageous as you wait on the Lord.***

I believe that I shall look upon the goodness of the LORD in the land of the living! Wait for the LORD; be strong, and let your heart take courage; wait for the LORD!

Psalm 27:13–14

7) ***Even if your situation feels hopeless, know that nothing is impossible with God.***

For nothing will be impossible with God.

Luke 1:37

8) ***You will never be lacking. God will supply all of your needs.***

My God will supply every need of yours according to his riches in glory in Christ Jesus.

Philippians 4:19

9) ***No matter what you are going through, you cannot be separated from God's love. His love is constant and never changes!***

Who shall separate us from the love of Christ? Shall tribulation, or distress, or persecution, or famine, or nakedness, or danger, or sword?

Romans 8:35

10) ***Wait patiently during this time of darkness. Know that God holds you and is making your steps secure as you seek joy and peace.***

I waited patiently for the LORD; he inclined to me and heard my cry. He drew me up from the pit of destruction, out of the miry bog, and set my feet upon a rock, making my steps secure. He put a new song in my mouth, a song of praise to our God. Many will see and fear, and put their trust in the LORD.

Psalm 40:1–3

REFLECTION QUESTIONS

1. Is there any area in your life where you feel stuck?

2. Look carefully at your life. We all have the same number of hours in a day. Where is all your time going? Like money, once our time is gone, it is gone. So we need to budget our time like we budget our money—wisely. Reflect on this past week. In what ways did you live wisely? Was there anything you did that was unwise?

3. What changes do you need to make in your life with how you spend your time? Are you staying up too late? Is technology on your phone or television stealing your

time? Do you need to work a little harder and more diligently so you can get things done faster and have time left for other priorities in your life? Where is all of your time going?

4. Are you putting your relationship with God first and seeking his will for your life? If not, what needs to change so you can seek God more?

5. Consider, are you waiting on God or is God waiting on you? Read Revelation 12:10–12. How does this passage of Scripture encourage you?

15 Finding Joy When Life Is Not Enjoyable

Prayer Journal Entry: Friday, February 3rd, 2017

What a mess of emotions I am wrestling with today! I can't stand the direction my life has taken. Oh, God, stop the crazy train, please. Every morning I wake up to this nightmare. I'm tired of praying, hoping, hurting, worrying, loving—I'm battle weary . . . I need rest. I need to enjoy life.

I Need to Enjoy Life

I was desperate. How in the world could I enjoy life when I felt like nothing was enjoyable? The word *enjoy* has the word *joy* tucked into it. If you were to continue to read on in my journal, you would see things did not get better. For the next few months I was on the struggle bus, but by the end of 2017, I was done with it.

I was sick of living miserable.

The tone in my journal completely changed as I decided I was going to choose joy. I got fierce about it and intentional. I sought wisdom and literally reorganized my life. I threw things out and cleaned up my eating. I began focusing on creating space and margin in my life to simply rest. I began listing all the things I was grateful for each day. I changed my habits because, friend, show me your habits and I'll show you your future. Change comes when we change our habits.

I Fought for Joy

And I won.

It's like a fire was lit in my soul! A genuine change took place in my life as the darkness lifted and I began to experience joy when nothing felt enjoyable. I was done being a victim, and it was time for me to show up to my life and live in the present without letting the past haunt me and the future scare me.

That summer I decided to do something brave.

I found a cheap hotel, and for the first time in my life, I drove alone—just me and the two kids—twelve hours to Myrtle Beach. The first night there I sat with my son out on the balcony as the ocean rolled in and out and the moon shined brightly over the water. We were quiet. Literally not a word was said as we sat there, and then my son began to cry. I cried too. Life was different without daddy there, and we felt the heaviness.

There it was again. The darkness was coming for us. It followed us all the way to Myrtle Beach, but no way was I going to let the enemy steal our joy this time! After that first night, we dried our tears, and this mom gave those kids the best of herself. We played together in the sand, collected seashells, threw the football, went on long walks, and adventured further than I ever would have before. We made fast friends with strangers on the beach. My kids played with their kids, and their dad took my son out in the water. God provided.

Every night I sat the kids down on the bed and we read the Bible together. Before we left home, I had prepared daily devotionals for our vacation. I'm a teacher at heart, so I took a poster board in my suitcase and hung it on the wall with sticky tack and pulled out my Sharpie. I know I'm a little extra when it comes to Bible study, but luckily my kids humor me.

I had clips cued up on YouTube of preachers to play for them. The kids watched the videos and then we discussed them. God was there, and he was helping our new little family move forward together.

I was growing stronger.

We got home from the beach, and there were big decisions to be made. Should I sell the house and move or try to stay? I prayed. I wrote the list of the pros and cons in my journal. I prayed some more. It felt like a huge decision with repercussions on both sides of the coin. I did not know what to do. No one else could make this decision for me. It was me and God battling it out. I was desperate for answers and scared of both decisions. The pros won, so I went to work changing the wall colors throughout the house. On the first floor, the original colors were dark burgundy, dark green, and gold. I was getting rid of the darkness, and that included those wall colors. I changed them all to white.

Living Loved

Long before my husband left, I had learned that life was hard. A full schedule, long to-do lists, and stress have always been a part of life. I had learned to sow seeds of joy into my daily life by lighting a candle and putting fresh flowers in the kitchen. I returned to playing soft music in the home and taking bubble baths. I used these as reminders to pray and rest in God's love for me. It was time, time to return to these daily habits, and as I did them repeatedly, I found a new rhythm in the home.

The darkness was being pushed out by the light.

Since the kids' father lived out of town, they weren't at his house every weekend like some children from divorced homes. So when they did visit their dad from time to time, instead of being sad, I savored the time alone. I watched movies, ate popcorn, walked the dog, went window shopping, and literally drove with no plan in mind. I wandered in my own hometown. I drove to multiple local lakes and sat on the docks and looked at the water and watched the boats for hours. I thoroughly enjoyed my time of rest. When it got cold, I continued my rhythm of rest. I sat in my car and looked out over the water and just simply breathed.

I was alone, but I was not alone. God was with me, and the more I lived in the present and acknowledged his presence, the more the darkness lifted. I could feel his love.

God was doing a new thing in my life!

As I implemented change, change was happening. You see, nothing will change if nothing changes. So I kept moving forward with change. My kids' father had really bad seasonal allergies, so we always kept the windows closed year-round for him. Now that he was gone, my dad came over and helped me put screens in every window of my home. Then we opened the windows and let the fresh breeze flow through the house. It was fabulous! I could hear the birds chirp, the rain hitting the pavement, and the crickets at night. It was all joyful music to our ears. We left those windows open day and night for weeks, and we loved it!

> See, I am doing a new thing!
>   Now it springs up; do you not perceive it?
> I am making a way in the wilderness
>   and streams in the wasteland.
>
> Isaiah 43:19 NIV

God continued to do new things in my life!

I was living loved. I was letting the simple gifts that God gives us each day through his creation be my joy. Life was becoming more enjoyable.

I heard a pastor once say that change only comes when we get sick and tired of ourselves. When the pain of staying the same is too great to bear. That was where I was at. I had spent a lot of time trying to change someone else—their father. But I can't control others, I can only control myself. So if he wasn't going to change, I was!

Friends, if something isn't right in your life, fix it!

Have you been stuck for years? Maybe you have been stuck in an area of your eating or organization. Same. I struggle with these things too. Satan wants us to feel trapped and like change will never come. Do not believe his lies. God did this for me, and you have the same God as I do. He will do it for you too if you will daily implement the change that is required for change. With God's help we *can* overcome!

Learning to Live the Abundant Life

During this time, I was still in hiding at my church. I attended the overflow service that met in the gymnasium. Every Sunday, as I sat in the service, I saw high up over my pastor's head these words written on the wall: "I came that they may have life and have it abundantly" (John 10:10).

There were weeks that I didn't hear a word the pastor said, and I just sat there thinking about the first half of this verse that says, "The thief comes only to steal and kill and destroy" (John 10:10).

Before I started moving forward, I thought, *It feels like the devil's winning. He is stealing and killing and destroying things in my life.* And I wondered, *What does an abundant life look like?* because I looked around and I knew that other people in my church were facing all sorts of suffering and sorrows as well.

Does the abundant life that Jesus promised include no struggles? Because we know that all throughout the Bible and history, Christians around the world have suffered.

I'm reminded of Hebrews 11:35–38:

> Some were tortured, refusing to accept release, so that they might rise again to a better life. Others suffered mocking and flogging, and even chains and imprisonment. They were stoned, they were sawn in two, they were killed with the sword. They went about in skins of sheep and goats, destitute, afflicted, mistreated—of whom the world was not worthy—wandering about in deserts and mountains, and in dens and caves of the earth.

Is this the abundant life that Jesus promised?

You see, even while nothing on the outside is enjoyable, the joy of the Lord is possible. It is a supernatural joy that this world cannot offer. The abundant life is not about financial wealth or earthly comforts—it's about the rich blessings we receive from God because of the gospel truth and because of our intimate relationship with him.

Abundance Equals Fullness

Are you full?

We have full calendars, full closets, and full trash cans, but what about our hearts?

For those who truly love God and live the uncompromising life of following Jesus, our lives are full. Our lives are full of faith, full of forgiveness, full of grace, and full of triumph over guilt and sin. Those who are walking in the Spirit will experience the fruit of the Spirit and will be full of love, full of joy, full of peace, full of patience, full of kindness, full of goodness, full of faithfulness, full of gentleness, and full of self-control (see Galatians 5:22–23). No amount of money can buy this fullness!

Praise Is an Underused Tool to Fight Back the Darkness

It can be challenging to pray long, read God's Word long, and praise long. We can be focused inward even when we are praying. But praise pushes out the negativity as we turn our eyes to the Lord. It refreshes our spirits. When life is not going your way, get on your knees, put on worship music, and push back the darkness. It was after my personal times of praise that I would rise refreshed.

One of the reasons we don't have a fullness of joy is because we don't take the time to enter into his gates with thanksgiving (see Psalm 100:4). The Bible says weeping may last for the night, but joy comes in the morning (see Psalm 30:5). It does not say that tomorrow morning your troubles will be gone but that tomorrow morning you will experience God's joy again. As sure as morning always follows night, so does joy always follow weeping. The psalmist also says to God, "in your presence there is fullness of joy" (Psalm 16:11).

So many times we've heard the Christian cliché, "God has a wonderful plan for your life." In times of heartache it can sound trite, but may we always remember that God *does* have a wonderful plan for us!

That does not mean that life will always be comfortable and easy, but it does mean that, in the end, the enemy who is trying to steal, kill, and destroy loses! And it also means that the abundant and rich gifts of the Holy Spirit are ours right now.

Psalm 65 says that the hills, meadows, and valleys shout and sing for joy out of their overflow of an abundance of grain and flocks. May we shout and sing for joy too! Our God is taking good care of us with more than just food and water—he has forgiven our sins and calls us his children!

I pray it is said of us, "*Nothing gets to that girl! She is always rejoicing and standing rock steady.*"

Joy Thieves

In closing, let me warn you to watch out for these little joy thieves. If scrolling on social media is stealing your joy, make a change. Stop scrolling. If eating a midnight snack is stealing your joy when you stand on the scale, make a change. Go to bed earlier.

You may be tempted to think, *I'll be happier when . . .*

- my kids are a few years older
- I get out of debt
- I have a new car
- I can finally go on a vacation
- my job changes
- my husband changes
- ____________________(insert your deepest longing and desire).

This type of thinking will make you *unhappy*! Destination thinking is a dead-end road because even when you get that thing you think will make you really happy, you will start to long for the next thing.

So it's time today to experience the fullness of the joy of the Lord. Joy is not a feeling, it's a decision. If something is coming to mind that you know needs to change, today is the day!

Change will not come easy, and the enemy will fight against you, but be relentless in your fight for joy. Remember that people will fail you, money may run out next month, you might have a midnight binge, and the rain might come inside those open windows and drench your carpet. Setbacks happen. But there is always a new day coming when we can find joy once again.

Enjoy God

Our God is fascinating—just look out the window and you can't miss it. Enjoy a beautiful sunset, the gentle breeze, the soft rain, the little caterpillar on the sidewalk, the birds chirping, the field of wildflowers, the squirrels gathering their nuts, and the rivers and streams in your area. It's okay to take an hour and just drive with your windows down and wander. If you have little ones, put them in the car and take them with you on the adventure. Put on songs of praise and point out all of God's goodness to them.

When reading Scripture, oftentimes we quickly jump to the application process, but there is so much to be discovered about the character of God from simply reading it. The deeper we go into the Bible, the more deeply we will know God and the deeper our joy becomes. His Word reveals his character, and when we know and understand his character, we will trust in him more.

God loves you. Live loved, stand firm, and remember—in his presence is fullness of joy.

Here Are Fifteen Verses about God's Character

1) **God is love.** ***God is the creator of love, and it is because he first loved us that we love others.***

For God so loved the world, that he gave his only Son, that whoever believes in him should not perish but have eternal life.

John 3:16

2) **God is faithful.** ***His love never ends.***

The steadfast love of the Lord never ceases; his mercies never come to an end; they are new every morning; great is your faithfulness.

Lamentations 3:22–23

3) **God is strong.** ***Our God is mighty. Find comfort in his strength.***

Seek the LORD and his strength; seek his presence continually!

1 Chronicles 16:11

4) **God is unchanging.** ***God is consistent and reliable.***

Jesus Christ is the same yesterday and today and forever.

Hebrews 13:8

5) **God is patient.** ***If God seems silent, it doesn't mean that he is not there. He has a plan and purpose and is patient to fulfill his will.***

The Lord is not slow to fulfill his promise as some count slowness, but is patient toward you, not wishing that any should perish, but that all should reach repentance.

2 Peter 3:9

6) **God is powerful.** ***No one can reproduce the mighty works of our God.***

He is the radiance of the glory of God and the exact imprint of his nature, and he upholds the universe by the word of his power. After making purification for sins, he sat down at the right hand of the Majesty on high.

Hebrews 1:3

7) **God will never leave you.** ***God's thoughts of you are immeasurable. They are precious.***

Keep your life free from love of money, and be content with what you have, for he has said, "I will never leave you nor forsake you."

Hebrews 13:5

8) **God is everlasting.** ***God is self-existent, and he is not just the creator of the world—he created you!***

Have you not known? Have you not heard? The Lord is the everlasting God, the Creator of the ends of the earth. He does not faint or grow weary; his understanding is unsearchable.

Isaiah 40:28

9) **God is giving.** ***God knows our likes and dislikes. Every gift comes from above.***

Every good gift and every perfect gift is from above, coming down from the Father of lights, with whom there is no variation or shadow due to change.

James 1:17

10) **God is perfect.** ***God's Word is true, and we can trust in him as our shield and refuge in times of trouble.***

This God—his way is perfect; the word of the Lord proves true; he is a shield for all those who take refuge in him.

Psalm 18:30

11) **God is a provider.** ***Do not give way to fear. God will meet all of your needs!***

Look at the birds of the air: they neither sow nor reap nor gather into barns, and yet your heavenly Father feeds them. Are you not of more value than they?

Matthew 6:26

12) **God keeps his promises.** ***What he says he will do—he does.***

God is not man, that he should lie, or a son of man, that he should change his mind. Has he said, and will he not do it? Or has he spoken, and will he not fulfill it?

Numbers 23:19

13) **God is merciful.** ***We will never have to face his wrath. He has forgiven us of all our sins.***

But God, being rich in mercy, because of the great love with which he loved us, even when we were dead in our trespasses, made us alive together with Christ—by grace you have been saved.

Ephesians 2:4–5

14) **God is a refuge.** ***God is always with us, guarding us and protecting us. We can rest easy at night knowing that our future is in God's hands.***

Trust in him at all times, O people; pour out your heart before him; God is a refuge for us.

Psalm 62:8

15) **God is holy.** ***God wants his people to speak of his mighty power and proclaim his name to all the earth.***

And one called to another and said: "Holy, holy, holy is the LORD of hosts; the whole earth is full of his glory!"

Isaiah 6:3

REFLECTION QUESTIONS

1. In what area of your life do you need God to do a new thing? Satan wants us to feel trapped and like change will never come. What changes can you implement today so you can experience more joy tomorrow?

2. Is your heart heavy right now? Perhaps you need a praise session with God. Think back and tell of a time when your heart was heavy and praise lifted your spirits.

3. Look in your Bible at Psalm 65. List all the things that the psalmist praised God for.

4. Do you struggle with destination thinking? John 10:10 says that the thief comes to steal, kill, and destroy. We must be aware of his schemes. What joy thief do you need to rid your thoughts of today so you can experience the abundant life that God has for you?

5. Psalm 16:11 says in God's presence there is fullness of joy. How often do you just sit in God's presence and enjoy him? Look out the window or go outside into his creation, and go into his presence now in prayer and pray Psalm 65 back to God.

PART 4

WOUNDED WARRIOR

1 The Spirit of the Sovereign Lord is on me,
because the Lord has anointed me
to proclaim good news to the poor.
He has sent me to bind up the brokenhearted,
to proclaim freedom for the captives
and release from darkness for the prisoners,
2 to proclaim the year of the Lord's favor
and the day of vengeance of our God,
to comfort all who mourn,
3 and provide for those who grieve in Zion—
to bestow on them a crown of beauty
instead of ashes,
the oil of joy
instead of mourning,
and a garment of praise
instead of a spirit of despair.
They will be called oaks of righteousness,
a planting of the Lord
for the display of his splendor.

4 They will rebuild the ancient ruins
and restore the places long devastated;

they will renew the ruined cities
that have been devastated for generations.
5 Strangers will shepherd your flocks;
foreigners will work your fields and vineyards.
6 And you will be called priests of the LORD,
you will be named ministers of our God.
You will feed on the wealth of nations,
and in their riches you will boast.

7 Instead of your shame
you will receive a double portion,
and instead of disgrace
you will rejoice in your inheritance.
And so you will inherit a double portion in your land,
and everlasting joy will be yours.

8 "For I, the LORD, love justice;
I hate robbery and wrongdoing.
In my faithfulness I will reward my people
and make an everlasting covenant with them.
9 Their descendants will be known among the nations
and their offspring among the peoples.
All who see them will acknowledge
that they are a people the LORD has blessed."

10 I delight greatly in the LORD;
my soul rejoices in my God.
For he has clothed me with garments of salvation
and arrayed me in a robe of his righteousness,
as a bridegroom adorns his head like a priest,
and as a bride adorns herself with her jewels.
11 For as the soil makes the sprout come up
and a garden causes seeds to grow,
so the Sovereign LORD will make righteousness
and praise spring up before all nations.

Isaiah 61 NIV

16 Church Wounds

We all have been wounded. No one gets through life unscathed. No one. When people we love, who are supposed to love us back, hurt us, betray us, reject us, or abandon us, it can take months and sometimes years to recover. The enemy loves to use our relational wounds to knock us down and keep us down.

You see, when God seems silent, it is hard. When we are overwhelmed with fear, anger, sadness, and other emotions, it is hard. Finding peace when there is none is hard. Finding strength when you feel tired is hard. Finding contentment with the woman in the mirror is hard. Getting unstuck and enjoying life when life is not enjoyable is hard. But friend, I saved woundedness for these later chapters because it can be beyond hard to recover at times, and it is vital that we learn to allow God's light to shine into the dark areas of our soul where we feel hurt.

I am the master of hiding and building walls. After trusting so many times and getting hurt, I have had moments when I've made a pact with myself to never trust anyone ever again. Have you been there? I had a moment when I decided to not give any private details about my life to anyone ever again. I went into protection mode, and it worked for a little while, but eventually it was a lonely place to live. Let me save you time—don't try it. It does not work. It is mentally, emotionally, and spiritually unhealthy, and so I had to figure this out. I had to read God's Word and let his light shine into my darkness. I had to learn to forgive, to trust, to let go of my bitterness, and to learn healthy boundaries so I could keep standing for another day. So let's get started. First up, church wounds.

It was 1995. I was away at college when my mom said on the other end of the line, "There's trouble at church. We might be leaving."

What?

The church I loved? The one where I had spent all my junior high and senior high years learning and growing in Christ. These were my most profound years of growth in my spiritual walk that led me to go to Bible college.

Leaving?

My safe haven away from public school. The place where I sang songs of worship with my best friends, went on mission trips yearly, and learned how to share my faith. The place where I sat in the pew and heard the Word of God preached boldly. The place where my brother-in-law was the junior high youth pastor. The place where both of my sisters got married. The place where I learned to serve in children's ministry, memorize verses, perform skits, and play games, and where I brought unsaved friends and watched them get saved—my beloved church.

My home away from home was crumbling.

I was away at college, and some of my friends from my youth group were also attending the Moody Bible Institute. We all were in shock. We loved our home church. There was a meeting being held on a weeknight regarding the issues, so we piled into a friend's car and drove seven hours to get to this meeting. It was sad. Very sad.

That night after the meeting, I walked out through those double glass doors for the last time—never to return. We drove through the night to get back to classes at school, but my heart was back in my old church.

Overnight it was just gone. I longed for what had been and was no longer there. Hundreds of people left the church, including my family. Friendships were torn in two between those who stayed and those who left.

I lost close friends that day.

I had always worshiped with my entire family, and even within our immediate family we were not all headed to the same church following the split. My brother-in-law was without a job. My other sister's husband was feeling led to return to his old church, and so our family was split.

Beauty from Ashes

> He has sent me to bind up the brokenhearted, to proclaim freedom for the captives and release from darkness for the prisoners, to proclaim the year of the LORD's favor and the day of vengeance of our God, to comfort all who mourn, and provide for those who grieve in Zion—to bestow on them a crown of beauty instead of ashes, the oil of joy instead of mourning, and a garment of praise instead of a spirit of despair. They will be called oaks of righteousness, a planting of the LORD for the display of his splendor.
>
> Isaiah 61:1–3 NIV

A few weeks later about five hundred of us would gather at a local public school and start a new church. This is the church I now attend. It has tripled in size, and it is beautiful. A God-fearing, Bible-preaching church. But the transition hurt, and our family still suffers at times when I miss my middle sister sharing a pew with us.

It's funny—even though this happened almost thirty years ago, the tears flow easily when I remember back to what was. The loss is real. The consequences of sin, pride, and quarreling rippled through friendships and families and still carry hurt today.

I love my church.

My beautiful broken church.

Church Hurt

Sometimes the church wounds, and those wounds leave scars. Over the years, I have had my fair share of squabbles, confrontations, hurt feelings, rude remarks, and judgmental comments. It's not fun. I've wrestled through how to be kind, how to hold my tongue, stay, and not run away and keep on loving, and sometimes I've failed miserably to do those things.

I understand the feelings of being a victim of someone else's gossip, slander, and betrayal. I have messed up too. Trusted friendships have been broken. Even after all of this, I still love my church.

We are all just sinners, saved by grace—nothing more.

I could post a bunch of verses about love and how the world will know we are Christians by our love, but I really don't think we need to read another verse about love. We know God commands us to love one another; it becomes a mere veneer to talk and talk about it. Sure, we can talk about loving the widow, the orphan, the poor, our enemy, each other, our community, but doing it—letting God's love fill the hard spaces between sisters in Christ—that is what's real.

You know what else is real? The enemy.

He is a roaring lion seeking whom he may devour. He hates the church. He hates you and he hates me. If we knew each other, he would want us to dislike each other, judge each other, have petty arguments, talk behind each other's backs, and never pray for each other. He hates our pastors, he hates our children, he hates our friendships, and he hates our love for the world. We must be aware of his schemes and push back the darkness.

Sadly, I think I could write an entire book on church hurt. I'm not exaggerating. The stories would be plentiful. When you stay in one place as long as I have and you've gone from season to season to season, it leaves a lot of room for wounding. I've gone from being a toddler to a teenager to married, having my own toddlers and my own teenagers, while teaching women's studies, being married to a deacon, and having a public ministry. While there were many bumps in the road through those seasons, nothing compares to the pits I faced when my husband left me and I became a single mom.

The years and layers of opinions toward me run deep in my church.

Insults hurt from those outside the church, but inside the church, the wounding can hurt so much more deeply. The reason is because the church is meant to be a safe place.

Over the years, I have experienced a lot of hurt from my church family. I suppose it's because I trust the people in my church and have assumed that if we are all following God's Word, wounding should not happen. But it does. Why? Because the church is filled with sinners, and the reality is we fail each other. And that includes me. I haven't always handled all my bumps and pits as well as I should have. I do have regrets.

Sadly, I started out as a teen too naive and too trusting. I have assumed good in people who were not as good as I thought. I lived life with arms wide open, and as a result I allowed myself to get stabbed in the back—and the front.

Friendship Fallouts in the Church

At a school event where my now ex and his mistress stood holding hands, a friend from church walked up to me (with my daughter standing beside me) and commanded me to take my husband home!

As if I could.

I told her, "I can get him home, but he won't stay." I had accepted him back eight times. I think he had a fair chance to turn himself around. I did not want the divorce, and I was not the one who filed. I forgave him over and over and prayed for God to save our marriage, fully believing he would.

She knew this.

As soon as she heard of our separation, she quickly invited me out to lunch and quizzed me about how I was handling my separation. She gave me instructions on how to fix it, though she had never been in this situation before. She was very black and white, and I had already tried everything she advised.

Here's the thing. I know in the church everyone says repeatedly "God hates divorce," but for some people in the church, it feels like they have reworked that verse into "God hates people who are divorced." Which is not what the Bible says. These are the verses that pastors quote when they say that God hates divorce. Let's take a look at the context.

> But did He not make them one, having a remnant of the Spirit? And why one? *He seeks godly offspring.* Therefore take heed to your spirit, and let none deal treacherously with the wife of his youth.
>
> "*For the Lord God of Israel says that He hates divorce, for it covers one's garment with violence,*" says the Lord of hosts. "Therefore take heed to your spirit, that you do not deal treacherously."
>
> Malachi 2:15–16 NKJV, emphasis added

Right before God says he hates divorce, he says he desires godly offspring. God sees and knows exactly what divorce does to the wife and children. He says it is violence against us. Divorce hurt us terribly. The struggle is real. God says it is real.

What I really needed from my friend was love and support while I went through the darkest season of my life.

She unfriended me on Facebook. It was baffling. If I'm confused by this behavior, I am sure that those who are unbelievers are confused by the behavior of some in the church as well. And often it's the reason they want no part of Jesus.

Where do we go from here?

I invited this friend for coffee and asked what I could do to make things better between us. She told me I needed to respect her right not to be my friend anymore. And so I must accept that.

You see, as believers we have two options. One, love your neighbor. Two, love your enemy. I'm not sure which of those we are, but one thing I know for sure is that for me, love is the only option. "By this everyone will know that you are my disciples, if you love one another" (John 13:35 NIV).

Conflict in the church is to be expected. We all have different personality types, family backgrounds, church backgrounds, sensitivities from our past, talents, giftedness, dreams, goals, fears, convictions on gray areas, theological leanings, political views, and life struggles.

Reread that list. That's a lot of differences! So as we come together, if we do not have humility and love we will clash like cymbals. "If I speak in the tongues of men and of angels, but *have not love*, I am a noisy gong or a *clanging cymbal*" (1 Corinthians 13:1, emphasis added).

And when we clash it is not pretty. It hurts.

This is what the Lord has taught me as I move forward in the church with my wounds:

1. It's okay to cry, but after I dry my tears, I must release the hurt to the Lord.
2. Think more about what Christ has done *for* me and less about what others have done *to* me.

3. Do not seek revenge. Christ paid on the cross for all my sins and all the sins done to me. Leave the sin of others at the cross for God to deal with.
4. Moving on is an ongoing process. When we see the face of someone who has hurt us, we may struggle again to forgive—we may have to continue to forgive over and over and over.

> Then Peter came to Jesus and asked, "Lord, how many times shall I forgive my brother or sister who sins against me? Up to seven times?"
>
> Jesus answered, "I tell you, not seven times, but seventy-seven times."
>
> Matthew 18:21–22 NIV

Moving on is not:

1. Necessarily a response to an apology. They may never be sorry.
2. Denying or minimizing what happened. It hurt, it was very real, and Christ died a horrible death to cover it.
3. Trust or reconciliation. It takes two to reconcile. When there is no acknowledgment of the pain they have caused you, you cannot be reconciled or trust them again. This leaves an open wound that only Christ can fill.

What if we don't move on?

1. Bitterness will grow in our hearts. Ephesians 4:31 says, "Let all bitterness and wrath and anger and clamor and slander be put away from you, along with all malice."

Reread the above verse. *All* means *all*. All bitterness, all wrath, all anger, all clamor, all slander, and all malice must be put away from us. That is a tall order, but God tells us to do this because he is protecting us from the pain that comes from these behaviors. It will eat us alive! We must not let the darkness win.

2. Our true character is revealed. Ephesians 4:2–3 (emphasis added) says we are to live "with all humility and gentleness, with patience, *bearing with one another in love, eager to maintain the unity* of the Spirit in the bond of peace."

Ephesians 4:31 shows us what we are *not* to be. Now look at this beautiful list in verses 2 and 3 of character qualities that come from standing in the light. We are to be humble, gentle, patient, loving, unified, and peaceful.

We have some work to do, don't we? Unity is not just for those who think and act and look just like us—that is self-idolatry. We are to work to *maintain* the unity of all of those in the church.

So how do we handle criticism when it comes?

1. Examine your own life, your motives, your intentions, and your heart, and compare it with the accusation. Is there any chance you are missing something that this person is pointing out to you?
2. Consider whether the problem is a personality difference, theological difference, philosophical difference, or a result of sin.

We see theological differences being worked out in Acts 15. We also see philosophical differences in the friendship of Paul and Barnabas. These godly men had a sharp disagreement and separated as a result.

> Some time later Paul said to Barnabas, "Let us go back and visit the believers in all the towns where we preached the word of the Lord and see how they are doing." Barnabas wanted to take John, also called Mark, with them, but Paul did not think it wise to take him, because he had deserted them in Pamphylia and had not continued with them in the work. They had such a sharp disagreement that they parted company. Barnabas took Mark and sailed for Cyprus.
>
> Acts 15:36–39 NIV

I really clung to these verses when I experienced a ministry split that was completely a philosophical issue, much like Paul and Barnabas's separation. I'll save that story for another day, but I just want to share that at the time of the division, I felt awful that two mature believers could not work out our differences and find unity. I could not have imagined the outcome at the time.

Division is a form of subtraction. I felt like I had suffered a great loss at the time. But now I see it less as a division, and instead multiplication has taken place. Both of our ministries have gone on strong. Multiplication is a form of addition. God was multiplying our ministries through our division. And I think the other leader and I would humbly agree that we both made mistakes and just couldn't do ministry together anymore, and though it felt quite sharp at the time, God was in it, and it was for the better for both of us and for the kingdom.

3. Grow thick skin. As Ephesians 4:2 says, "[bear] with one another in love." Sometimes we simply have to put up with and tolerate a person who rubs us the wrong way for the sake of unity.

My Wounds Have Changed Me

One temptation is to become jaded. To wonder if putting myself out there is worth the hurt. It makes me want to crawl into my bed, cover my head with my covers, and never come out again. It makes me want to push everyone away and never trust anyone with my heart ever again.

This is what the enemy wants—a severely wounded, jaded Christian who is unable to serve or love again.

But God.

God spoke into my darkness and reminded me that he is sovereign and in control. Though I've been surprised by my wounds, God is not. God has allowed all the difficult situations in my life for a reason. God is taking me deeper in with him, to trust him more and love him more. To change me not into a jaded person but into a compassionate person who identifies with the wounds of others.

> Blessed be the God and Father of our Lord Jesus Christ, the Father of mercies and God of all comfort, *who comforts us in all our affliction, so that we may be able to comfort those who are in any affliction*, with the comfort with which we ourselves are comforted by God.
>
> 2 Corinthians 1:3–4, emphasis added

Have you been wounded?

The enemy wants to isolate you from the family of God. He wants you to throw in the towel and leave the church. Don't do it! Remember, we are all just sinners, saved by grace—nothing more. "For it is by grace you have been saved, through faith—and this is not from yourselves, it is the gift of God" (Ephesians 2:8 NIV).

It was hard to share everything in this chapter because I know some in my church might read this. But I wrote it for the woman who might be feeling jaded or hurt today. I pray you would allow God's light to shine into your wounded darkness. Let God heal your wounds and then turn them around and use them to comfort others. That is how we triumph over the enemy!

REFLECTION QUESTIONS

1. In what ways have you been wounded by the church? How does remembering that we are all just sinners, saved by grace, encourage you?

2. Read Ephesians 4:31. Has anything on this list tripped you up? Now read Ephesians 4:2–3. Which of these character qualities do you need help on developing more in your life?

3. Think for a moment. Name a person who irritates you or simply rubs you the wrong way. Ephesians 4:2–3 says to bear with one another in love and maintain unity. How can you live this out?

4. Is there someone in your church you need to forgive? Read Matthew 18:21–22. What does Jesus say to do?

5. Second Corinthians 1:3–4 says God comforts us so that we can be a comfort to others. How have your wounds made you a more compassionate person?

17 | Friendship Wounds

Friendships among women are not easy. Why? Because the enemy is not going to let them be easy. He does not want us to experience love. He hates love. In the heart of every woman is a natural longing to connect and belong, and so the enemy is going to do everything he can to make us feel disconnected and like we don't fit in. He wants us to try to play it safe by building walls and creating boundaries so we end up living in isolation. Any animal that is chasing his prey is going to go after the vulnerable one that has been separated from the pack.

Do not get isolated.

We need each other. Think of a single spaghetti noodle before it's been cooked. It is easy to snap and break. Alone, a noodle is weak, but when you put a group of them together, suddenly those noodles are strong! If you have ever tried to break a bundle of them to put into a pot of boiling water, then you know it takes real effort to snap a group of noodles. Like the noodles, together we are stronger. The enemy knows this, and so he wants to divide us, isolate us, and push us into darkness.

But, friend, we must fight back. We must help each other to keep standing!

I know this is easier said than done. You see, I'm a social butterfly. I'm also an introvert. I'm what they call an extroverted introvert. A social dichotomy. I love to be alone and read and write. I do not like to be interrupted when I'm in deep thought, and I need space. I enjoy shopping alone and eating alone. I can go for days without leaving my house and be very happy. But I also love to travel and go to new places and meet new people. I enjoy talking, laughing, shopping, and eating with my friends. I enjoy family get-togethers, and sometimes I'm the last to leave. I love one-on-one time with my friends where we can go deep, but I'm also of the mindset *the more the merrier*. So the more people gathered, the more excited I get about our time together.

When I was younger, I had no idea friendships could end. For some reason, I imagined that all the friends I made I would keep. I would love them, and they would love me—forever.

I was wrong.

I learned the hard way that friendship breakups are very painful, especially when someone knows you inside and out.

It all began in junior high when I had friendship bracelets with two girls. The three of us were best friends, but three became a crowd. It always felt like one of us was left out. That fizzled, and it was sad. Then in high school I received a best friend necklace. I had half a heart on my necklace, and she had half a heart on her necklace. The necklaces could have been an omen of our friendship, signifying that eventually we'd break each other's hearts in two, and we did. Our friendship ended when our church split.

Then in college, I made new friends. They were amazing, and I thought for sure those friends would be forever. I mean, we lived together for four years in the dorm and shared such sweet times of fellowship together, but after graduation we all went different ways. I lost touch with most of them. Seasons continued to change through multiple moves, multiple jobs, married life, and becoming a mom, and my friendships became like a revolving door.

I never did like revolving doors.

Love Is a Risk

Friendships are a risk. The older we get, the scarier they can be. Bumps, bruises, and scars from the past can make it hard to take the risk of making a new friend. And that's just what the enemy wants you to believe. He wants to isolate you and get you alone. That is the easiest way for him to take you down.

One of the reasons I started accountability groups called Good Morning Girls groups was so women would not be alone. They were meant to give women a safe place from the world, where sisters in Christ could openly share, be encouraged, and be loved. We need each other!

Thousands of women across the globe are in Good Morning Girls groups today, but the enemy does not let up. Even right in my own group the darkness threatens to tear us apart. Little misunderstandings can creep in if we are not careful, and over the years, my group has hurt people's feelings who are not even in our group. I had no idea this was happening until someone told me they felt excluded from our group because they were not invited to be a part of it. I certainly did not want my Good Morning Girls group to feel like an exclusive club, and I felt awful.

You see, sometimes we are the ones doing the wounding. I am far from perfect, and I know I have hurt others. I am not proud of everything that has ever left my mouth. I have said some things over the years that should not have been said, and so I recognize that as much as I long for unity and love, I have hurt others.

When Friendships End

While I wish no friendships ever had to end, there are some friendships that just simply must end. Once someone shows you who they are—believe them. The ones who say "I just don't get along with most girls" are most likely going to be a problem for you. Or the ones who say "I just say it like it is" are most likely going to be rude to you. I don't want rude friends. I don't like to feel confused with my emotions and wonder if I am overreacting or if they are just mean.

If every one of their friendships before you fell apart, what makes you think you will be the exception? If they have had consistent drama with everyone, it won't be different for you. I have sat and replayed conversations in my head, wondering how they went sideways and if things could be repaired. I was offended, and so were they. I apologized, and so did they, but things are just not the same anymore.

Now, don't get me wrong. I have a few amazing lifelong friends. I recognize they are gifts from God and not everyone has friendships that have lasted since their teenage years. My issue seems to be that I want every single friend I've ever made to stay a lifelong friend. So I am always disappointed and hurt when one of my friends disappears out of my life, especially if that disappearance was preceded by conflict.

Healing the Wound

It is only natural to run from pain. If I see a bumblebee, I'm going to run from it. But unlike physical pain that stops when the thing hurting you stops hurting you, emotional pain can go on for years. And so we must not run from the pain. Instead, I'm going to ask you to revisit your wound, because the only way for a wound to heal is to properly care for it. Think back to the wounding:

- Who hurt you?
- What were the circumstances surrounding the fallout or wounding?
- What was said or done that feels almost unforgiveable?
- What have you turned to as relief from this pain and heartache? Is the thing you have turned to healthy and good or unhealthy and toxic?
- How did friends and family respond to this season of loss? Were they supportive, or did they add to your pain?
- Are you still holding on to the pain and nursing this wound?

Now that you have looked directly at the wound, let's look at what God has to say about those who mistreat us.

> You have heard that it was said, "Love your neighbor and hate your enemy." But I tell you, love your enemies and pray for those who persecute you, that you may be children of your Father in heaven. He causes his sun to rise on the evil and the good, and sends rain on the righteous and the unrighteous.
>
> Matthew 5:43–45 NIV

Love your enemies.

Pray for those who mistreat you.

Pray. Pray. Pray.

In Matthew 9:12, Jesus presents himself as the great physician. He came for the sick. When my kids went to the orthodontist, the work he did to straighten their teeth hurt them. But it was a good pain. He was helping them. In the same way, it may be painful to obey God and pray for those who have mistreated you, but he wants to heal you, and forgiveness is the only way. He does not want you to suffer in bitterness.

> Make every effort to live in peace with everyone and to be holy; without holiness no one will see the Lord. See to it that no one falls short of the grace of God and that no bitter root grows up to cause trouble and defile many.
>
> Hebrews 12:14–15 NIV

You see, when we pray and are in God's Word, our heart becomes more like God's heart. God's heart is full of mercy and grace toward us, and so the closer we are to him, the more grace and mercy we can give others.

Forgiveness Is Not a Feeling

What I won't ask of you is to feel a warm fuzzy toward this person who has hurt you. That is not what forgiveness and freedom look like. It is not a feeling. And though God is a God of reconciliation, he is not asking you to be reconciled to them. Some people are unhealthy, and you must protect yourself from them.

What I want for you is healing. I want you to actively push out the darkness and be free! The best thing for you is to let this open wound heal and become a scar. You see, scars are something that we carry with us for a lifetime. They remind us of the pain we have experienced, but they don't hurt anymore when you touch them.

Ask me how I know?

The *other woman*—was a friend.

I knew her for ten years before she became the *other woman*. We had gone on multiple trips together; she had been in my home, and I had been in hers. We had done lunch together one-on-one. My kids knew her kids and vice versa. I liked her. I liked her husband. I liked her kids. I never in a million years imagined the way she would wound me.

She has unapologetically cut me to the core.

And the wounding did not stop after the divorce was final. The ripple effects of her choices will last a lifetime for me, but with God's help, biblical forgiveness is possible, and to be honest . . . I didn't do it for her. I did it for myself. I fear God. I don't want to be sideways with him. Jesus said, "Forgive, and you will be forgiven" (Luke 6:37 NIV).

I want to forgive because I want to be forgiven. Or let me turn that around: I love because he first loved me. "We love because he first loved us" (1 John 4:19 NIV).

Jesus went first. He set us free from the power of sin by his death on the cross. He wants us to live free. If we don't learn how to let other people's sins roll off us, then their sins will hold power over us and we will not be free.

I did not like the way the enemy was using the other woman to hold power over me. And I do not like the way the enemy is using that person who wounded you to have power over you. In the next chapter I'll talk about how to let it go, but for now pause, step out of the darkness, and step into the light. Forgiveness is a decision. Decide to forgive, not for their sake but for yours.

REFLECTION QUESTIONS

1. Who hurt you? What was said or done that feels almost unforgiveable?

2. Why is it important that we seek healing from the wounds others have inflicted upon us?

3. Read Hebrews 12:14–15. What does bitterness cause? How can we avoid bitterness from developing in our lives?

4. Our enemies are not usually at the top of our prayer lists, but Jesus tells us to pray for our enemies and to pray for those who mistreat us. Write a prayer for your enemy.

5. Forgiveness is not a feeling. It is a choice. It is a matter of our will and of trusting that God knows what is best for us. Who do you need to release feelings of resentment toward and forgive? I'm so sorry for the way they have hurt you. God sees and he cares. Choose to forgive them today. Now write the date that you made this decision.

18 Letting Go of Your Hurt

I tried.

I don't regret it.

A lot of people thought I was crazy for taking my husband back multiple times. According to Matthew 19:9, I had biblical grounds for divorce. I could have filed immediately, but I didn't.

Instead, I prayed. I prayed that he would repent and come home. Then I waited. And he came home and left and came home and left. It got dark and messy. He sent me an email on Valentine's Day with terms for a dissolution. Legally, a dissolution is the same as a divorce. The only difference is rather than using lawyers to divide the assets, together we sat at the kitchen table and did the dividing. This included parenting time. After we came to an agreement, he filed it with his lawyers, and six weeks later we appeared in court to make the divorce final.

That email with the terms for our dissolution was quite a contrast to the Valentine's Day just one year prior. I still have pictures from that day. He had given me a dozen roses, chocolate-covered strawberries, and had written on the card,

"You are the best wife in the world. I love you forever."

Forever?

After he left, I looked everywhere I could for clues that this was coming. How did I miss all the red flags? Instead, what I found was evidence of his love, which only confused me worse.

He and I had dated long-distance for four years in college. We wrote love letters to each other every single day for those four years. I am not exaggerating. I have hundreds of handwritten love letters from him in my closet, and we continued to write love notes to each other once we were married. I found an anniversary card he gave me a few years prior. He wrote:

Courtney:

Happy Anniversary my love! I love you more than ever before. Your beauty grows greater the closer I am to you! You are the best! You bring joy, happiness and fulfillment to my life! You are awesome. I would marry you 100x's again if given the chance. I Love you dearly!

I found a Mother's Day note from him and the kids, written in his handwriting:

Five Things that make you the <u>best</u> (the word best *was underlined twice) mom/wife in the world . . .*

1. Teaching our kids about Jesus

2. Loving and forgiving us when we are not good

3. Good communication with all of us

4. Supporting our interests . . . work, karate, gymnastics, flying

5. Giving us all the things we need . . . food, clothes, love, friendship

We love you
mommy!!!!

I had notes like this tenfold in the closet. I had saved them all over the years. I just could not believe he really had stopped loving me. How did we get there? Nothing felt like it added up. Did I even know what real love felt like? How could I be such a fool?

I loved him more than anyone else in the world. We got along well and did not fight often. Don't get me wrong—we did fight, and it was not pretty when we did. Now that we are not married, I do see some of the unhealthy patterns we developed in our marriage, but I did not see this coming nor did anyone else. And so I tried. I tried to keep my marriage together, and I don't regret it.

Follow the Instruments

After our dissolution was finalized in court, we continued to get back together and separate. He stayed in our finished basement, and we talked about remarrying. Then he took me and the kids to his new home a few states away. The last night that I was there, I left him a note on the nightstand. I don't remember everything I wrote, but I did end the note by saying, "*Follow the instruments.*"

John F. Kennedy Jr. was a pilot. Late one night he was flying over water, and he experienced spatial disorientation. He got confused as to which way was up and which way was down and crashed into the water, killing himself along with his wife and her sister. Had he followed the instruments on his dashboard, he would have known his plane was upside down, but he followed his feelings and they cost him his life.

My now ex-husband has been a pilot since he was a teenager. We had flown many times together, including over the ocean. He is the one who told me the story about John F. Kennedy Jr. and about the importance of following the instruments rather than his feelings when he flies.

The day I left his home a few states away, I knew he was deeply confused and disoriented. I also knew that if he followed God and God's Word and not his feelings, our family would be saved. And so I wrote these words in my final love letter ever written to him: "*God's Word is your instrument. Follow the instruments.*"

Life Is Hard

Some days are harder than others. The fear, worry, pain, and stress can be too much to bear, and then I am reminded to give it to Jesus. "Cast all your anxiety on him because he cares for you" (1 Peter 5:7 NIV).

Jesus told us to give all our burdens to him, and yet for some reason I think I can carry my burdens quite well on my own. I work hard to manage my pain. I want to carry it well. But this is worldly thinking. We aren't supposed to be carrying our burdens alone. Jesus tells us to give him our burdens.

What Are You Holding On To?

You see, if I handed you a filled sixteen-ounce water bottle and told you to hold it out in front of you for ten seconds, you could do that with no problem. If I told you to hold it out in front of you for a minute, it might feel like a challenge, but you could probably do that as well. Now, if I told you to hold that water bottle out in front of you all day long, your arm would get tired and sore, and it would eventually hurt you.

This is exactly what we do with our burdens. We think they are small. We hold them for a little while and we seem fine, so we keep holding them. But then over time we hold them longer and longer, and somewhere in there we start to get grouchy and irritable or perhaps sad and anxious, and we wonder why we don't feel right.

Our pride tells us to keep pushing through it, and so we act like our burdens are not hurting us, but they are.

We need to stop.

We need to humble ourselves and release our burdens to Jesus.

What are you holding on to?

Why are you holding on to this thing?

Answering the *why* is much more difficult than the *what*. The why is our motivation. We need to identify our motivator. We all have different motivations for not letting go of things. Maybe we want to be in control, or maybe we fear what will happen if we let go. Perhaps you are like me, and you don't want to feel like a failure. When it comes to committing or signing up for something, I'm not a quitter. So if I commit to something, I do it. This means I need to not commit to too many things at once.

Maybe you are gripping something tightly out of fear of suffering loss. Perhaps you fear a financial loss and are in a job that has gone sideways, and you need to leave. Maybe it's moving to a different home or different church, and you are scared.

If it's a relationship—and I've done this—maybe you are holding on to a ghost from the past. You have sweet memories with this person, but your present reality is that this person has changed, and you are having trouble accepting that.

Acceptance and surrender are where you will be healthy. Holding on to dead things is like gangrene. Gangrene can make you sick. You must cut it out, but cutting off an unhealthy relationship is very painful and hard. So perhaps you live life in limbo, always suffering under the surface. Friend, the quickest way to healing is to release that thing to the Lord and let yourself grieve the loss.

Maybe you are a perfectionist, and you cannot calm down until all your ducks are in a row. The problem is, life will never be perfect, so you might feel like a hamster on a wheel getting nowhere fast. Or maybe you are unhappy with yourself right now. Perhaps you are trying so hard to make a change and reach a certain weight goal, and that goal is weighing you down. It's another day, another month, another year of not reaching your goal, and it feels hopeless.

Perhaps you have a child who is wayward, and it would feel like you were giving up on them if you stop doing whatever you are doing that is not working. You are not God. You cannot change people. Only he can change them.

Then there's lack of forgiveness. Perhaps you've been wounded deeply by someone you love, and you have grown bitter. You replay the hurtful words and memories over and over and get angrier the more you think about it. You are holding on to a grudge, and it is hurting you.

Release It All to God!

You may be thinking right now, *I know what I'm holding on to, and I know why I'm holding on to it, I simply don't know how to release it, Courtney.*

Friend, some of these issues are dire. I hope in desperation you will heed these words of wisdom I'm about to share with you and find healing.

Let me show you how to lay it down.

If my little toddler was holding a knife with the sharp edge in the palm of her hand, I would not pull it out of her grip by the handle. It would cut her. Instead, I would say, "Open your hand, honey, and let Mommy have the knife before it hurts you." Once her hand was open, then I would take it from her, and she would be safe.

You and I are the toddler. That thing we insist on carrying around is the knife. We are holding on to things that we know can hurt us. The tighter we hold on to them, the more pain we are going to experience. The more we tell God no and refuse to give up that knife, the longer we are going to suffer. Until we willingly open our hand up and let God take it from us, we will continue to experience pain.

He will not take it from us.

He will not rip it out of our hand.

He is waiting on you to release your grip and surrender it to him.

I can testify that peace, freedom, and rest are on the other side of surrender. We have a God we can trust. He knows the details far better than we do. He is incredibly faithful. He will never leave us. Our God loves you deeply, no matter what you have done, good or bad. And so when you trust him with every fiber of your being, you will realize the safest place to be on earth is surrendered to him.

Surrendering control does not mean things will all turn out with rainbows and butterflies. I am not living in all the ideals that I dreamt of living in when I got married.

But I am free.

I have joy and peace from God inside my heart. And no one can take that away from me. A Scripture passage I have turned to time and time again for encouragement during times of surrender is Psalm 121:1–5, which says:

> I lift up my eyes to the hills.
> From where does my help come?
> My help comes from the Lord,
> who made heaven and earth.

He will not let your foot be moved;
  he who keeps you will not slumber.
Behold, he who keeps Israel
  will neither slumber nor sleep.

The LORD is your keeper;
  the LORD is your shade on your right hand.

God does not sleep. He sees and knows all. He knows exactly what is burdening you right now. He knows that you don't want to let go of it, and he knows your why. He wants you to trust him. Look to the hills. He made them, and he made the heavens and the earth. He will help you.

Open Your Hand

Like the water bottle, it might seem small, and you might wonder if you really do have to let it go. I can testify, it will wear you down.

Open your hand. Let it go.

Like the knife, maybe this thing you are holding on to is terribly painful. I can testify, you will continue to live like a wounded bird if you do not let go.

Open your hand. Start the healing process.

We will talk about this more in the next chapter. But for now, remember, God loves you. He laid down his life for you so you could lay down all your burdens before him. Keep walking with the King.

REFLECTION QUESTIONS

1. What are you holding on to?

2. Is the thing you are holding on to more like a water bottle or a knife?

3. Determine your why. Why are you holding on to this thing?

4. Read Psalm 121:1–5. Make a list. What do these verses teach you about God, and how are they a comfort to you?

5. Now look at the list you just made. Pray these verses and this list over your life, and surrender the burdens you have been carrying to God right now.

19 Recovering from Loss

I remember sitting and listening to an older woman in our church share about her cancer journey. She said she felt like she was on a train headed one way, and when she found out she had cancer it was like her train had been derailed. Suddenly she was in a foreign land with foreign people. She was meeting new doctors and new nurses and learning a foreign language of medical terms related to cancer.

As I sat there and listened, I felt the same way. When I was married, my life was headed toward all my hopes and dreams. Suddenly, my husband left, and my life was derailed. Now I was headed to a foreign land of divorce, trauma, brokenness, singleness, grief, and many other new losses. I entered a foreign world of new books and podcasts. New people came into my life, like counselors, and women who were also divorced tried to help me. There was a new language with new topics that I needed to learn.

Before my train was derailed, a writing mentor of mine had made some comments that made me doubt whether I could keep writing after my husband left. Those words rang loud in my mind after my husband walked out the door. I almost quit. But the Lord wouldn't let me. He continued to give me words in season and out of season, and so I kept writing, and one day this comment appeared on Instagram.

> "Thank you for holding fast to the Lord despite your struggles. Your attitude in these past 3 years is the best sermon you have ever preached. Well done."

This commenter will never know the encouragement and healing she gave me that day.

Healing from Loss

Healing takes time, and waiting on time to pass is not something any of us enjoy. Most of us prefer to keep busy as time passes. But working through grief requires slowing down and giving yourself time to feel your sorrow. Grief can feel like a hard stop and an interruption to our lives. When we do stop, we do not know what to do with our sadness and anger, and as believers we might even feel guilty for not having the joy of the Lord. This causes us to keep pushing forward and to fake fine when we are not fine.

Do not fake fine.

We must allow ourselves the space and time to grieve our losses. You see, we cannot heal and mature without slowing down and working through our pain. Just like the trees that lose their leaves in the fall, the leaves do not return quickly. It takes time, and if a tree buds too early in the spring and the snow falls again, it will damage the tree. We cannot try to bloom too soon.

We must give grief time.

The Five Stages of Grief

To recover from our losses, we need to allow ourselves to work through the five stages of grief described in the Kübler-Ross model. If at any point we get stuck in a stage or we do not allow ourselves time to work through the emotions we are feeling, our body will know it. We will feel sick, anxious, have headaches, be irritable, or for years appear fine on the outside until one day it catches up with us and we are not fine. So let's look together at the five stages of grief.

Stage 1—Denial

In this stage, you will be in shock and disbelief that what is happening is really happening. There will be people in your life who will very quickly want to shake you and get you into reality and out of denial, but God uses this denial to protect you.

Without denial you would be flooded by more emotions than you could possibly handle at once. Denial gives you time to mentally process your pain so you do not absorb it at an intensity that would normally overwhelm you. This stage is a hidden blessing at the start, but we cannot stay in denial. We must keep moving forward if we want to heal.

Stage 2—Anger

In this stage, you will feel angry at the situation that has been forced upon you. You may ask the question *Why?* over and over. You may have moments of rage at the situation, at God, or at the person who caused your pain. God uses this stage as a form of protection for you as you begin to move out of denial and feel the intensity of your loss.

This can be a very lonely place to be. The people around you may try to spiritualize your problem so that you stop being angry, or they may condemn you for feeling angry. But it is healthier to let your emotions out than to hold them in and grow bitter. During the anger stage, I ran harder on my treadmill than I ever had before or since. Channeling your anger into a sport, a hobby, or music is a healthy way to move through this stage. It is only natural to protest our losses, but we must not stay stuck in this stage. We must keep moving forward if we want to heal.

Stage 3—Bargaining

In this stage, we may try to do anything we can to get out of the pain we are in. We are no longer in denial, and we have suffered through the anger stage and now are desperate to be done. We want to put our sadness and anger to rest the quickest way possible, and we want to regain control of our lives. We want our sense of normalcy back, and this could mean either returning to a toxic situation, making life-altering decisions when we are not thinking clearly, or trying to bargain with God that if we do a certain thing, perhaps he will give us a different outcome.

While all of this may seem unhealthy, God uses this stage to give us glimmers of hope as we hang on for dear life during the hardest season of our grief. When the reality of the loss remains, and nothing we try to do is removing the pain, oftentimes hope is lost and we very quickly move to the next stage.

Stage 4—Depression

In this stage, we experience deep sadness, loneliness, and displacement. This is a very quiet stage of withdrawal where we may spend hours, days, or even months sleeping, crying, and reflecting on the deeper things of life. We may wonder how we can go on or what the purpose of life is.

God uses this stage to help us face the reality that the person or situation is gone forever. Normalcy is lost during this stage, but that is making way for new patterns to develop. Friends and family may be worried and hope you snap out of it soon, but it's important that they consider the question "Is she facing something that is genuinely depressing?" And if the answer is yes, then it is best that they let you be sad and sit in that sadness with you. I remember getting to a point where I felt cried out. I literally could not cry another tear over my losses, and it was at this point that I was ready to move forward into the next stage.

Stage 5—Acceptance

Acceptance is the final stage of grief. It's at this stage that we experience healing. You will literally feel different inside and have hope for a brighter future. Though you may be triggered and cry at times over your loss, the loss is no longer dictating your day-to-day emotions. You may never be the same from your loss, but you move forward with peace and accept that you cannot change what you've lost. It's at this point that we reconfigure our life, and as we figure out our new reality, we feel stronger as we begin to enjoy life and laugh again. We can see that we are going to be okay.

Acceptance is unlike denial in that it doesn't pretend the loss hasn't happened but rather you have worked through all the stages and emotions of that loss, and now you are ready to live life forever changed and better for what you have been through.

It's in this stage that we are ready to move forward full of hope. God uses this stage in our lives as a testimony and comfort to others. Others can see how God has brought us through and how he has restored our joy and they are encouraged.

Grief in Bible Times

The way people grieved in Bible times is significantly different from how we grieve today. It's interesting to note how much time and outward expression was devoted to their grief. Scripture says they tore their clothes and put ashes on their heads (Esther 4:1). Then they put on sackcloth and wept and wailed. People took off their jewelry, and women were called to come and cry loudly with those who were mourning (Exodus 33:4, Jeremiah 9:17–18). Whole communities mourned together for thirty days (Numbers 20:29), and some communities stopped eating and fasted for seven days together (1 Samuel 31:13).

I think we could stand to learn from how grief was expressed in the Bible. Their culture left room for them to publicly feel their feelings. Their communities showed up, and they cried together. I love that! I wish I had experienced something like this. I know that divorce is different from a death and that some communities do mourn deaths well. And I recognize there's secrecy and a gossip circle that makes the loss of a husband through divorce messy. I mean, nobody is planning a meal train for the woman whose husband just left her. So it's just plain awkward for everyone, but the grief is just as real. My family would testify that my grief oozed out at the most inopportune times, and looking back at it, most likely it was because I truly needed people to just sit and cry with me over my losses. I lost a husband, a daily father to my children, my provider, my protector, and my best friend.

I tried so hard to control my emotions, but it didn't really work.

My Final Outburst

I spent a solid three years in the grief cycle. I remember very clearly being back in the bargaining phase of grief for the sixth, seventh, or maybe eighth time. I lost count at some point.

It had been a year since I left that handwritten note on the nightstand. It was Father's Day, and my children's father was pursuing me to reconcile, but everything he said felt wrong. My gut knew I could not go through the disappointment of this not working out again, and so I put some conditions in place to protect us. He was immediately angry with me for those conditions and stopped his pursuit. And just like that I fell into grief immediately, only it was time for me to go to my sister's house for a family get-together to celebrate my father on Father's Day.

No one in my family knew what had just happened hours previously, and so I walked into that family get-together faking fine. Two hours later, I would literally be lying on my sister's staircase coming completely undone as if someone had stabbed me in the heart. I have no clue what I said that day to my sisters, but I was angry at my situation and I was sad and I was desperate for relief from my pain. I could barely even breathe. I sobbed loudly, and I am sure my family was exhausted with my saga, but there I was, a very broken woman who could not fake fine another minute.

That day was a monumental day for me. I think I cycled through every single one of the stages of grief in one day. That was my final outburst. After that, I was calm, and I accepted that my marriage of nineteen years was really over.

Different personalities go through each of these stages differently and with different intensities. Some of us regress and must go through a few of these stages over and over before we leave the cycle and enter the acceptance phase.

That was me.

When we step back and read through the stages, we can see how God uses each of these stages in our lives to move us forward. But when we are in the midst of emotional flooding, nothing makes sense. Things will happen that trigger emotions out of nowhere, but you can know that healing has taken place when you reach a point where those emotions flood you and you do not lose hope. You know that joy is coming after your tears. Your happiness is no longer tied to that person or thing you lost.

Follow the Man of Sorrows

In Isaiah 53:3, Jesus is called "a man of sorrows and acquainted with grief."

Jesus knows our pain. He sees it all, and he cares.

> He was pierced for our transgressions,
> he was crushed for our iniquities;
> the punishment that brought us peace was on him,
> and by his wounds we are healed.
>
> Isaiah 53:5 NIV

He wants to heal us from more than our grief and sorrow. He wants to heal us from our sin. Through our faith in him we have hope. We have hope of a resurrection and life in heaven with him because Jesus's death on the cross brings victory over darkness and death!

Revelation 21:4 tells us that one day Jesus will wipe every tear from our eyes. There will be no more death or mourning or crying or pain in heaven. What a wonderful hope this is! And so when we grieve, we do not need to grieve as the world grieves without hope (1 Thessalonians 4:13).

We will always carry the pain of our loss with us, and at times the calendar will be relentless as it reminds us of birthdays, anniversaries, the day things went downhill, or the day we lost our loved one.

But there is always hope with Jesus.

Life is full of new beginnings even when we are old. So take courage. Be strong. Be present and feel your feelings, and then let your losses go and stand firm in your faith. God loves you.

REFLECTION QUESTIONS

1. Have you ever felt like your life has been derailed? Like you were headed one direction and then suddenly you were forced to go a different direction? What happened?

2. Is there something in your life you have grieved or need to grieve? Look over the five stages of grief. What stage are you in right now?

3. How does grief in the Bible look similar or different to how you have experienced grief?

4. Read Isaiah 53:3–5. How do these verses describe Jesus?

5. Read Revelation 21:4. What hope does this verse give you?

20 Still Standing

Since my kids were ages ten and twelve, I've been a single mom. Being a single mom is hard.

It's like playing a game of tag and always being *It*. A child needs help with their homework, I'm *It*. A child needs a ride, I'm *It*. A child needs to be disciplined, I'm *It*. A child needs to learn to drive, turn in college applications, get ready for prom, go to the doctor, or get a haircut. I'm *It!* I've always felt a step behind and like there was a huge gap in our lives.

But by the grace of God—all glory to him alone—I'm still standing.

Spiritual warfare is real. The enemy has come at me from every side, and I have my battle scars to prove it. The enemy's grip on me was tight.

But God

God's grip on me is tighter.

He is the rock at the bottom when the bottom falls out.

He is my refuge and strength, a very present help in times of trouble (Psalm 46:1). And because he is my refuge and strength, because I am trusting him with my future, because no matter how bad life here on earth gets I know I have the promise of eternal life in heaven through his son, Jesus Christ—because of this truth, I know everything is going to be okay.

I mean, life has not been okay. But I have experienced 1 John 4:4 (NIV): “You, dear children, are from God and have overcome them, because the one who is in you is greater than the one who is in the world.”

Our God is greater! And so we can keep standing!

A Beautiful Family

I tried to hide at church, but God saw me. We can’t hide from God. In his sovereignty, he used my hiding in the gymnasium worship service to plant me one row behind this beautiful family. There was a father, mother, their two daughters who were in their twenties, and a fiancé. They were far down the row in front of me, so we never met.

Fast-forward five years. My sister sent me a message I still have on my phone today, asking me to pray for this family. The wife was in the hospital dying, and so I prayed. A few days later my sister sent me a second message telling me that the wife had passed away.

I looked at the date.

The Date Was December 22nd

I swallowed hard. That was the exact same day five years earlier my husband had left me. My heart went out to this man whose name I did not even know until my sister messaged me to pray for the family. How was it possible that his wife died on the same day my husband left me?

What an odd coincidence.

That following Sunday we all sat in the same spot, only the wife was not there. My heart broke for them. After the service, people gathered around the family as they hugged and comforted them, and I watched from a distance not knowing what to say or do. Then I stepped forward and tapped the younger daughter on the shoulder, and I told her I had been praying for them. She looked at me with the most beautiful smile and said, "Thank you, Courtney."

She knew my name?

I did not know hers.

She was smiling through her tears.

The darkness had pressed in on this family, but they were still standing!

My heart went out to the husband, who had just lost his wife the week of Christmas. I knew how painful that was. I asked my sister for his name; she answered, "Keith."

My children's father's name is Keith.

What an odd coincidence.

Week after week, I watched this family come into the service and stand and sing to the Lord, sometimes with their hands raised. Then they would sit with their Bibles open, listening to the sermon. When the service ended, they would visit with the people around them, and I noted their warm smiles despite their deep loss. We never spoke, but I did notice how handsome Keith was and that he was still wearing his wedding ring.

Eventually, they would move to the sanctuary to worship, and they would be out of sight and out of my mind.

Our First Date

It was late in the summer when another message from my sister popped up on my phone. She informed me that this man from church had asked her husband for my phone number, and he would be calling me soon. As my sister and I were typing back and forth, my phone began to ring.

It was him!

Nothing could have prepared me for what was about to take place. The first date was just for dinner, but it turned into a three-hour dinner. I don't think either of us wanted it to end. He was funny, talkative, warmhearted, hardworking, interesting, and he adored his children. I loved that! When he prayed over dinner, my heart soared. A praying man who takes initiative is a good man!

After a few dates, he made it clear he liked me, and I liked him back, but I explained to him that we could not date seriously. My children were sixteen and eighteen at the time, and I did not want to disrupt their final years of high school with my love life. They had already been through so much, and I wanted to protect them. He is a family man, and so he was very understanding of my needs as a mother.

His wife was his high school sweetheart, and he had not dated anyone else since she had passed away. My husband had been my high school sweetheart, and I had not dated anyone else since he left. And so we laughed at how awkward it was to be dating at our age, and I encouraged him to date around because I was not ready for anything serious.

He did not listen.

He kept calling and texting, taking me out, meeting my friends and family, and everyone loved him. He is literally one of the most outgoing men I have ever met in my life. He is friends with all of his neighbors and doesn't seem to meet a stranger. If he meets you once, he'll remember your name and all the details about you.

Falling in Love

About a month into dating, we went to a lake by my house and sat on a dock that I have sat on probably a hundred times alone to pray and meet with God. Never did I dream that I'd be on that dock with the man who sat one row in front of me in church.

It was a warm, clear night with just the moon and stars out. We sat side by side. As we looked out over the water, I began to ask him questions about the loss of his wife. He was very open, and he talked about his pain, loss, struggles, and grief. I asked him if the pain of his loss had ever caused him to doubt God. He quickly answered, "*No*." He said he fully trusted God and his faith had not wavered. He was thankful he knew she was in heaven and okay.

Literally every word he said that night I felt in my soul too.

I related to his grief over a lost spouse even though his wife had passed away and mine was lost to a divorce. We both loved our first spouse deeply. We both did not want our first marriage to end. My faith had not wavered either. I was holding on to God and not letting go, and so was he. We both had this in common, and that night I realized I was connecting with him in an area that I connect with no one else in my life. I have wonderful girl friends, but this isn't something we share. I knew that night I was falling in love. God was connecting our hearts together through our pain and loss, and he was a comfort to me.

Fast-Forward a Year

God did a lot in our first year together. We got engaged, broke ground on a new home, and together moved my son into his college dorm. Then, another year passed. Remember back when I told Keith after a few dates I would not get married until my kids had graduated? Well, the time has come! My daughter has now graduated, and as I am writing this, we are just three weeks away from our wedding. I cannot wait for the big day, and we are so blessed to have his son-in-law officiating our wedding vows.

I know this all sounds amazing, but let me explain how the darkness hovers even in the midst of our joy. Keith has moved into the new home with one of his daughters, and after the honeymoon my kids and I (and our fluffy white dog) will all be moving into the newly built home too. This may sound like our lives are being tied up neatly into a bow, but soon the For Sale sign will be in our yard, and we will begin the blending of two families.

One thing I have learned is that all blended families are born from loss. Moving into a new home together means we are closing the door on their childhood homes and the memories made there with their first families. None of them ever dreamt they'd see For Sale signs in their yards or be a part of a second family. This was the hand they were dealt, and this leads to a lot of hard things that first families do not have to deal with.

Change is hard, and tears are a part of moving forward. My heart breaks for everyone's losses, but this I can say, by the mercy and grace of God alone, all of the children are thriving despite the enemy's desire to take them down. I am so proud of them all and the way they have walked through their trials with such strength. It is not an accident that God has planted us all into a second family together. We are all fighters, and I don't mean with each other. I mean against the enemy.

What Hand Has Life Dealt You?

I know that your life may not be going the way you thought it would. It may feel like this dark valley will never end. It may feel like the battle is raging with no relief in sight. Be assured, God is with you. He is at work even when you cannot see it. This dark valley *will* end.

Do not be passive with the darkness in your life. I want you to live free. Though you cannot see it now, as you push back the darkness, you are growing stronger than you ever were before. You are going to finish well!

Look at the future hope we have in heaven:

> Then the angel showed me the river of the water of life, as clear as crystal, flowing from the throne of God and of the Lamb down the middle of the great street of the city. On each side of the river stood the tree of life, bearing twelve crops of fruit, yielding its fruit every month. And the leaves of the tree are for the healing of the nations.
>
> No longer will there be any curse. The throne of God and of the Lamb will be in the city, and his servants will serve him. They will see his face, and his name will be on their foreheads.
>
> There will be no more night. They will not need the light of a lamp or the light of the sun, for the Lord God will give them light. And they will reign for ever and ever.
>
> Revelation 22:1–5 NIV

In heaven, the darkness is gone! There is no need for the sun. There is no need for a lamp. God himself is the light. And we are his image bearers. We are the light of the world!

> You are the light of the world. A town built on a hill cannot be hidden. Neither do people light a lamp and put it under a bowl. Instead they put it on its stand, and it gives light to everyone in the house. In the same way, let your light shine before others, that they may see your good deeds and glorify your Father in heaven.
>
> Matthew 5:14–16 NIV

Let your light shine in the darkness. Your story and your testimony are needed to guide and comfort others.

Remember, on hard days, our God is a consuming fire. His kingdom cannot be shaken! "Therefore, since we are receiving a kingdom that cannot be shaken, let us be thankful, and so worship God acceptably with reverence and awe, for our 'God is a consuming fire'" (Hebrews 12:28–29 NIV).

And so my final words for you come from 1 Corinthians 15:58 (NIV): "Therefore, my dear brothers and sisters, stand firm. Let nothing move you."

Rise up.

Stand firm.

Let nothing move you.

Finish well as you walk with the King.

REFLECTION QUESTIONS

1. You are strong and you are still standing! How has God been the rock at the bottom when the bottom falls out?

2. Read 1 John 4:4. How is this an encouragement to you in the midst of life's challenges?

3. Look at the future we have in heaven described in Revelation 22:1–5. Write a list of the amazing attributes of heaven.

4. Matthew 5:14–16 says we are the light of the world. In what ways are you shining your light in this dark world?

5. Write out 1 Corinthians 15:58. Take time to memorize it and then pray it over your life.

ACKNOWLEDGMENTS

To my parents—You have taken every step of this difficult journey alongside me, and I cannot thank you enough for your unconditional love and support. During my darkest days you were there for me, answering the phone every time I called, loving my children over Sunday lunches, sending wisdom in encouraging emails, and praying never-ending prayers over me and the kids. I'm forever grateful, and I love you.

To Alex—Thank you for all the laughs and late-night talks. I have leaned on you during hard times, and you have been there for me and your younger sister. Your wisdom and understanding of life have been a comfort to me. You are smart and you are strong, Alex. Thank you for all your hugs, love, and support. You have made me a proud mama! I cannot wait to see what God has in store for you. I love you.

To Alexis—From sharing clothes and secrets to sharing ministry ideas, there is no end to the joy of the friendship we share. You may be the younger child, but you are still the big sister. Thank you for always being there for me and your brother. I am so blessed to have a godly daughter who truly lives out the joy of the Lord in her life. Your smile lights up every room you enter. I can't wait to see God's plans unfold in your life. Thank you to you and Anson for supporting me during the writing of this book. It means so much! I love you.

To Keith—Thank you for that first phone call. I never imagined I would get a second chance at love. I remember at the start, riding around in your red pickup truck on Fridays. I would look over and admire you as you talked, and then inevitably you'd say something hilarious, and I'd be laughing. You have changed my life. I can't wait to see how this next chapter of my life unfolds with you at my side. I pray he uses our story and our marriage for his glory. I love you, handsome.

To Ky, Jenna, and Charlie—Your father is the proudest father on the planet. He adores you all. Your strength and faith are amazing. Thank you for letting me be a part of your lives. I love hearing your stories and your perspectives. You have accepted me into your family, and I am forever grateful for your openness and kindness to me. I love you all.

To Kristen and Jennifer—I am double blessed to have two big sisters who love the Lord and follow hard after him. Thank you for supporting me through all the ups, downs, twists, and turns my life has taken. I am especially grateful for the way you have welcomed Keith and his children into the family with hearts and arms wide open. I love you both.

To my Good Morning Girls—Kara, Kelly, Kimmy, and Katina. You were there when the bottom fell out. During that time, I needed my girl friendships more than I had ever needed them before, and you all showed up in the most profound ways. I am forever grateful for your prayers and your listening ears. I love you all.

To Karen and Ruth—This book would not exist without you two. I am so grateful that God brought us all together many years ago through our ministries. But you are more than ministry partners; you are dear friends and confidants. Thank you for driving a long way to show up at my doorstep and cry with me. I am forever grateful for your encouragement and wisdom in my life. I love you.

To Rosilind—The world's best virtual assistant! I can't believe we have been doing ministry together for over ten years.

You have an amazing heart for the Lord, and the way you serve with joy is always an inspiration to me. Thank you, Ros, for all of your help. I could not do this without you! I love you.

To Jennifer Dukes Lee—My editor. Thank you for taking a chance on me and this book! It is an honor to write with you. I appreciate you.

To God—My savior and Lord. I am humbled every day by your kindness toward me. Thank you for using me despite all my mistakes and flaws. I love you, Lord.

NOTES

Chapter 1 Where Are You, God?

1. Elizabeth Gamillo, "An Estimated 50 Billion Birds Populate Earth, but Four Species Reign Supreme," *Smithsonian Magazine*, May 19, 2021, https://www.smithsonianmag.com/smart-news/50-billion-total-wild-birds-inhabit-planet-study-estimates-180977753/.

Chapter 2 Does God Hear My Prayers?

1. "H7210—rŏ'î—Strong's Hebrew Lexicon (KJV)," Blue Letter Bible, April 17, 2023, https://www.blueletterbible.org/lexicon/h7210/kjv/wlc/0-1/.

Chapter 4 Why Is Being Still Not Working?

1. "H5542—selê—Strong's Hebrew Lexicon (KJV)," Blue Letter Bible, April 17, 2023, https://www.blueletterbible.org/lexicon/h5542/kjv/wlc/0-1/.

Chapter 9 I'm So Worried

1. *Merriam-Webster*, s.v. "worry (v., n.)," September 10, 2023, https://www.merriam-webster.com/dictionary/worry#.

COURTNEY JOSEPH FALLICK is a bestselling author and the founder of Women Living Well Ministries and Good Morning Girls. A graduate of Moody Bible Institute, Courtney has been featured on the *Rachael Ray Show* and spoken at many national conferences, including Relevant, Allume, Proverbs 31 Ministries She Speaks, The Nines, Axis, Mom Heart, and Hearts at Home. She's been blogging through the Bible, one chapter a day, since 2014, and makes her home in Ohio with her blended family. Learn more at WomenLivingWell.org.